CANADA LOST
CANADA FOUND

CANADA LOST

CANADA FOUND

The Search for a New Nation

A Polemic by

Peter Desbarats

McCLELLAND AND STEWART

McClelland and Stewart Limited
The Canadian Publishers
25 Hollinger Road
Toronto, Ontario
M4B 3G2

CANADIAN CATALOGUING IN PUBLICATION DATA

Desbarats, Peter, 1933-
  Canada lost/Canada found

ISBN 0-7710-2682-X

1. Federal government – Canada.   2. Canada – Politics
and government – 1968-1979.*   3. Canada – Politics and
government – 1979-1980.*   4. Canada – Politics and
government – 1980-   *   5. Canada-Economic
conditions – 1971-   *   6. Canada – Social conditions –
1965-   *   I. Title.

FC600.D47   971.064'6   C81-094040-X
F1034.2.D47

Printed and bound in Canada

Contents

Author's Note

I could not have written this work in the limited time available were it not for the creative research effort of Betty Weinstein and the encouragement of Bill Cunningham, former Vice-President of News and Current Affairs at Global Television, whose convictions about journalism over the years have been unwavering no matter how the corporate winds blow.

This book belongs as much to my wife, Hazel, as it does to me. In our work together and our life together, she has made all the difference.

". . . one of the things I'll remember, and will probably be puzzling over as long as I'm able to puzzle, is the damfool way you keep spoiling life for yourselves, bringing out the worst in one another. There's so much good here, and you keep throwing it away. . . ."

Sinclair Ross
Sawbones Memorial

1.
A Time for Decision

So much nonsense has been written about us. We've preferred it to the truth. The truth will set you free, it is said, yet freedom is the one thing we have feared.

Comfort and safety have been our national objectives, within cages of our own making. Intrusions have been deeply resented. The freedom to be our crippled selves has been sacrosanct. We can hardly remember when it was any other way in this part of North America and we desperately want it to go on forever – desperately, because we know now that it can't. The cages are suffocating us. The flowing histories of other nations no longer swirl smoothly past us like crowds at the zoo. They are poking their fingers through the bars. We draw further within ourselves, trying to seek consolation in the old litanies of self-deception.

We have been called a nation of navel-gazers and we've accepted that description with a certain amount of pride, pretending that the study of ourselves is virtuous and productive. Introspection has become our most characteristic national activity, has developed into a national industry. Books, newspapers, and magazines describe us; television documentaries reflect us. Each latest production seems to be longer and more complex than the last. The process feeds on itself. The references to previous studies multiply like mirror images. As the documentation becomes more impressive, the findings and conclusions grow more elusive.

We're on the brink of that tragic moment when the footnotes become the whole story and our story becomes a footnote in history. We've studied our navels to avoid looking into our hearts. How futile! If we were truly discovering ourselves, the knowledge would liberate us; but our performance has declined as our self-analyses have multiplied.

Long ago, we lost the ability and the desire to rival the accomplishments of the past. Our ancestors now seem like giants; it's embarrassing to place their dreams beside our own pygmy aspirations, and so we rarely do it. Few nations quote the leaders of the past so reluctantly.

The failures of the present are harder to ignore. We still try to escape them by falling into the black holes of our various introspective national philosophies. We try to transform them into illusions of progress, spiritual if not material, but we grow impatient with our own trickery. Every area of national activity presents us with a never-ending panorama of missed opportunities, misguided and abortive enthusiasms, and vast potentialities that never seem to be realized.

What little success we do have is poisoned at the source. We finally achieve a flourishing movie industry in this country only to discover that all the stars are foreigners and most of the films are unbearable. This just happens to be a recent example. In many other fields, we have risen from national mediocrity to international irrelevance. With nothing meaningful to say to ourselves, we can scarcely expect to offer anything useful or even comprehensible to others.

We used to boast that we had the second highest, perhaps the highest, living standard in the world. The prosperity bestowed on us by nature gave us the illusion of progress. We might have been "a dull people enamoured of childish games," in the words of one of our poets, Irving Layton, but many other peoples envied us. Now we are said to be sixth or seventh and dropping further down the list. This is the crude measure of our relative decline.

Until recently, we've succeeded in concealing this failure from ourselves. We've been distracted by world conflicts, economic recessions, and other events outside our control. Now only a nuclear war would blot out our failure to mature as a nation. We live with this failure every day.

At the moment, it is oil that illuminates our weaknesses. By the gift of nature, we are relatively well-supplied with natural resources. We could have been virtually self-sufficient in energy if we had wanted to develop our resources to achieve this. Even now, we should be in a position not only to weather global resource shortages but to improve our relative position. Instead, we are tearing ourselves apart in an internal struggle over our own riches.

The principle that a single province of our Confederation should take precedence over the national government on questions of national development is not only advanced and debated but accepted and put into practice.

Fragmentation is our natural state. We don't know how it feels to be intact or to belong to a coherent and confident national society. We marvel at the way the British understand one another's jokes, at the way the Germans sing one another's songs, even at the way Americans fight one another. With us, learning to be different from one another starts at the beginning. Many of us were born in Protestant, Catholic, or Jewish hospitals. Even if those natal distinctions have largely become outmoded, most of our children still attend schools divided by language and religion and all of these various school systems exist within ten fiercely independent provincial systems.

We learn about divided loyalties when we learn how to read. The more we read about ourselves, the less we are able to perceive this as a problem. We transform it into a virtue, and thank God that the divisions within our country have saved us from the vices that afflict others.

"In our weakness and our diversity," wrote one of our political scientists, "we are saved from the temptations of aggressive nationalism."

When a nation seeks consolation in its disability, it does violence to its own spirit. And this is not the most ridiculous of the myths we have used to comfort ourselves. An entire generation, the most recent of those to head into oblivion without being able to stem or harness the destructive tides ripping through our country, defined itself as citizenry of an "unknown" country. In less than a century, according to this grandiose delusion, an unexplored country had become an incomprehensible nation. Too vast to understand.

Our own generation has taken comfort in the mere fact of survival. Or, to be more precise, in the possibility that perhaps we have survived. "Have we survived?" asked the poet Margaret Atwood. "If so, what happens after survival?" Our very existence becomes problematical and our future hypothetical.

This can't go on much longer. Many of us are beginning to sense that. Bad enough that we have started to seem ridiculous to outsiders; now we're also driving ourselves crazy in the literal sense, hardly able to find our real selves in all the rubbish we have thrown up to conceal the truth.

"Your very nationality," according to the New York Times, "consists of an identity crisis with which you have a national love affair."

Others think we must enjoy being like this. They now define us in terms of the disease that is destroying us.

One of our favourite pastimes has been to compare ourselves with Americans: "Is there really any difference?" The game lasts forever because we refuse to finish it. We compare hamburgers, soft drinks, cars, and television programs, then conclude that because these are the same we must be identical.

The game would have seemed ridiculous to our ancestors. They could tell the difference between a Canadian and an American: an American was the one at the other end of the rifle barrel. In their newspapers, caricatures of Uncle Sam or Brother Jonathan portrayed him as a sly and seedy Yankee trader. The caricature of Young Canada, sometimes male, sometimes female, was robust, attractive, filled with the strength of its own innocence. Now we laugh at these crude drawings, but the drawings themselves mock us. We are afraid to explore the fate of that potent idealism about ourselves. We prefer the superficial distractions of the American game, comparing vocabularies, table manners, and reading habits.

Let us compare histories. Let us compare mythologies. We have no common history with the United States. Our origins were different; our objectives were distinctive. Only when we failed and lost sight of ourselves did we turn to the Americans for solace. Americans were undisputed masters of the universe in those days and there was consolation in asking ourselves if we were like them and in pretending to discover that in some mystical way we weren't. These exercises in self-deception usually terminated in the discovery that we possessed most of the American virtues and none of their faults.

Americans also served us well as scapegoats, but this is so obvious it hardly needs saying. We added up the billions of dollars Americans poured into our country and drained out of it. We had objections to both activities, although never strong enough to discourage them. We counted up the hours we spent reading American magazines and watching American television. We devised complicated quotas for ownership, publishing, playing the guitar, acting, singing – all part of an extraordinarily difficult effort to stem the invasion. Sometimes we seemed to shore up our "Canadianism," but always in the same fragmented way: patching the holes in the dike while the structure crumbled and swayed over our heads.

It was always difficult because if we couldn't agree on why we were doing it, how could we agree on what to do? All the solutions seemed to violate something within us as much as they damaged the invaders. In fact, we were starved for freedom but also afraid of it, and the only way we could express this was by attacking the freedoms of others. That was the grotesque expression of the distortions we had wrought upon ourselves.

Our fixations about the United States simply puzzled the Americans themselves. Writing about this, his adopted country, an American academic who came here ten years ago, Edgar Friedenberg, responded to our apparent confusion about national identity by quoting something from his own folk wisdom: "There ain't, as the saying goes, any place anything like this place within miles of this place; so this must be the place."

In our heart of hearts, we know this but we haven't dared to acknowledge it. If this really is the place, then for generations we have tried to be someplace else.

Hundreds of thousands of us actually moved away. Someone has estimated that half of the descendants of a Canadian couple married in 1900 are now Americans. We fled in droves under the pressure of economic recessions, whether we spoke English, French, Yiddish, or Ukrainian, but always the flow was south and often it was the brightest and the best who went. More than money attracted them, as they sometimes tried to tell us, although we hated to listen to the other reason. It was freedom, expressed in many different ways. For the young, there was freedom to advance quickly in a society willing to take chances, freedom from the oppressive weight and tenacity of an older generation here that seemed to be afraid of anything that moved.

During the war in Vietnam, the cowardly, the confused, and occasionally the courageous came to our country in exchange for this traditional contribution of young, ambitious, and innovative spirits. Now our southerly exodus is over, partly because we have glimpsed a new appreciation of ourselves, largely because the Americans have almost closed the door on immigrants from Canada and we don't have, at least so far, the desperation, courage, and subversive skills of the Mexicans who continue to flood into the United States from the other direction.

As they say in Quebec, we now have to swallow our own spit. The turmoil in Quebec in the past few decades has been blamed partly on the closing of this safety valve. You can still find enclaves of French-speaking Canadians in the United States, the older ones in the mill towns of New England and the newer in the tourist mills of Florida and California, but exodus is no longer the prospect it used to be for a young

French-speaking Québécois. The same holds true for English-speaking Canadians who used to move freely into the work force not only of New York and Los Angeles but of London, Sydney, and other centres of the Commonwealth. Now we have to stay at home and take a hard look at what Canada is and has become.

Emulating, criticizing, or joining the United States have all been ways to avoid the proper study of ourselves. Now we are starting to see our own country. The myths are slowly disappearing and we are beginning to understand, for the first time in our experience, the extent of our failure. It is awesome and frightening, but at least it has the ring of truth and we can start to build upon it.

Quebecers are somewhat ahead of the rest of us in this because the gap between myth and reality was more extreme and first became intolerable there. Facing the truth in Quebec has been a traumatic process. Divisions between classes, generations, and language groups have been widened; the Quebec economy has been damaged; and reaction still threatens at times to overthrow the work of reform. Despite all this and beneath it all, a basic change has occurred in Quebec society and in the mentality of Quebecers.

We still find this strange in the rest of Canada but nothing exotic has happened in Quebec. On the contrary, Quebec has been attempting to return to normal after several centuries of conquest, oppression in one form or another, and failure to mature as a society. The rest of Canada didn't share the conquest or the oppression but it has shared fully in the failure to mature into a proper national community. Because of its more difficult history, Quebec simply became aware of the disaster before the rest of us did and was impelled to do something to try to save itself.

Quebecers were aware in recent decades that many other peoples were on the same road and they were encouraged by this. The rest of us still fear comparisons with other developing societies because we still harbour the illusion that we are an old and established country. We fear the comparison with newer communities that have sometimes progressed further in a few decades than we have in centuries. This state of mind is about to disappear in the rest of Canada for the same reason that it disappeared in Quebec twenty years ago: because the gap between illusion and reality becomes too great to sustain. We are forced to discover what we really are, no matter how painful it is.

It's a question of survival with self-respect. Once Quebecers saw themselves as they really were, they came dangerously close to losing all respect for themselves, their politicians, their institutions, and their ancestors. They glimpsed what it would be like to lose sight of the future. They had to change or to abandon themselves to despair.

Of course it doesn't happen all at once to everyone. There was a remarkable Scot at the National Film Board in the 1940's, its founder John Grierson, who described almost thirty-five years ago the mentality of a "subconscious" Canada that he felt was even more important than the face Canada then presented to the world. Grierson said there was "growing up swiftly in this country, under the surface, the sense of a great future and a great separate destiny." Grierson was uncannily perceptive about Canada, but the subconscious yearning he sensed in the country took decades to express itself and when it did, it happened in a form that would have horrified him.

So acutely were Quebecers struck by the realization of national failure, as they looked at themselves several decades ago, that many of them despaired. They struck out on a new course or, rather, an old path they had always known about but that few of them had ever followed. Many of them set out in this direction despite the fact that explorations of political independence in the past had either ended in disaster or simply petered out. That was the measure of their desperation. But they were armed, at last, with a true appreciation of themselves. That insured progress, no matter which path they chose. They changed their society. They radically altered their political system. They moved ahead, after centuries of stagnation, and that dictated changes for all of us.

It has been difficult and terrifying at times for many Canadians to be unexpectedly and often unwillingly caught up in this process. In other provinces, we were at different stages of development with different preoccupations. Only now are we beginning to understand that the process started in Quebec twenty years ago is part of a national process. It just happened to start first in Quebec.

Once it started, it moved quickly. The political and social metabolism of Quebec accelerated in the sixties until the province was out of synchronization with the rest of the country and proceeding rapidly at its own pace and in its own direction. If there was ever a time when we were close to being two distinct entities, this was it. Most intelligent, politically aware Quebecers felt that if the course of events continued in the same direction at the same speed, the federation with the other provinces would be ruptured and Quebec would have to find its own way.

Political developments, as we've all learned, rarely proceed in a straight line. There have been so many revolutions and counter-revolutions in Quebec in the past two decades that the population has lost count and almost lost interest at times. Among all the crises and turning points, the election of an indépendantiste government in 1976 seemed to be identifiable as a watershed event, but it was soon evident that the means used by the Parti Québécois to achieve this victory were more important than the end. Only the promise of a referendum had persuaded Quebec voters to trust the separatists, and the referendum soon overshadowed the existence of the Lévesque government and eventually threatened it.

The referendum campaign in the spring of 1980 was hailed as the most memorable political event of a generation. For once, the hyperbolic vocabulary of the news media will be repeated and even amplified by history. Many books eventually will recount the roles of Premier René Lévesque and Liberal Leader Claude Ryan and the sweep of the federalist majority across the province, but they will find it difficult to communicate the emotions that gripped Quebecers during the campaign.

So basic were the passions and sentiments that they remained hidden until Quebecers revealed them on secret ballots behind the screens in polling places across the province. Many people hesitated to place the blue "no" placards of the federalist side on their homes not only because of threats from their neighbours but because they didn't want to openly repudiate the feelings of the "yes" side. During the campaign, a journalist who accompanied a canvasser for the "yes" side on a survey of a street in east-end Montreal reported that the majority support for independence obtained by the canvasser was reversed the next day when she went over the same territory with a "no" canvasser. At issue were two different political expressions of Quebecers' new sense of self-respect. Those who supported the more complex expression enunciated by Claude Ryan understood and respected the simpler, more radical, and sometimes more aggressive position taken by Premier Lévesque.

The final political rallies of the "no" side stirred up emotions foreign to this generation of Canadians, not on the platforms but in the audiences. The platforms were dominated mainly by rows of political hacks from various parties who had spent most of their lives cutting up one another and who had every intention of continuing to do so. While these improbable temporary alliances signified the importance of the struggle, the audiences expressed what was really happening.

It was a matter of feeling and will. None of us had ever heard ourselves sing "O Canada" as fervently as during that campaign. Whether we sang it in English or French was irrelevant. The fact that the lyrics had no official status as our national anthem had no importance. When, the day after the referendum, the House of Commons voiced its approval of a motion urging the government to make "O Canada" the official national anthem, it simply affirmed our belief that we had now started to march far ahead of our politicians. There was pride among these Quebecers at being Canadian, all the more remarkable because it was being displayed in a province where many of us least expected it.

There we all were, joined together in a political exercise that all of us would once have considered unthinkable: a vote on the question of our continued existence as a nation. But as we drew closer to confronting this outrageous question, we became stronger nationally. The time had come to test our strength and Quebec was showing that we could do it with confidence.

On the day of the referendum, Quebecers dared to stand up and be counted. A majority voted for Canada. Despite the deliberately obtuse question, the issue was clear to everyone.

It might have been politically more astute for most Quebecers to have voted for the "yes" side. Lévésque then could have gone to Ottawa with a ticking bomb in his hand. Quebecers decided that the issue was too important for that kind of manoeuvring, traditional as it might be in Canadian politics. They gave a straightforward answer and waited for the response from the rest of the country.

That response is slow in coming but it's there. It has to be. The next and conclusive phase of the process will be based on the assumption that it is there, but this doesn't mean that the outcome is inevitable. Canadians outside Quebec have evolved more gradually in the past twenty years, and many of their preoccupations have been different. Because the process of completing the work of the first Confederation, the Confederation of 1867, happened to start in Quebec, there is a feeling that it is being forced on the rest of the country, rammed down our throats. Canadians in other provinces want to set their own agenda for national reform.

The fact is: this is the agenda that all of us have created. It is the outcome of our common history. No matter when we came to this country and declared ourselves to be Canadian, this is now our history and we will have to respond to it. It isn't going to be simple. We're all going to have to put aside old preconceptions about one another, and some of our attachments to the past, to create something new. The politicians, the news media, and all of us are going to have to try to control the conflicts inherent in this process. Once it really gets underway, divisions will widen for a time, old prejudices will be inflamed, and feelings will run high. Many of us will say it is un-Canadian, and it will be if our precedent is the failure of previous generations to come to grips with our problems and to liberate us from them. Many will want to turn back to a familiar haven, not realizing it already has disappeared. Each one of us will have to choose whether or not to accept the risks and to press ahead.

We are going to have to see Quebec, for once, not as the source of many of our problems but as the key to a solution. We are going to have to see that the conjunction of the Quebec problem and the Alberta problem at this point in history may be a blessing if we can make the right connections between the two. If Quebec, for instance, has compounded our difficulties in finding a national solution to our energy problems, it stands to reason that the road to accommodation with Alberta leads through Quebec. Once we start, we'll be able to see connections everywhere. What appears to be a contradictory array of isolated regional problems will be seen as expressions of problems common to us all, the result of our common failure to live up to the expectations of the creators of the first Confederation more than a hundred years ago. When we see that, the threat of a Québec Libre will transform itself into the promise of a truly liberated Canada.

Can we do it in the next few years? That's all the time we have because the next cycle of nationalism in Quebec, if we fail now, will be fearsome. Instead of starting with a few disgruntled souls, as this one did in the late fifties, it will begin with that 40 per cent "yes" vote in the 1980 referendum.

I know how exhausted all of us are. I feel like I've been writing about it forever. Our politicians are groaning inwardly with despair as they are caught up in the toils of yet another try at constitutional reform. But there is a difference this time, and it lies not in the mechanics of reform but in our own feelings at this point in our history *and* in our own determination to respond to that remarkable vote in Quebec.

I have a wonderful feeling, perhaps the nearest thing to something once called inspiration, that I am saying nothing new. There are no footnotes in this book because so many people are saying this in so many different ways. I have the feeling that I am simply stating what is in all our hearts, that within a few years this book will be regarded simply as a statement of the obvious.

2.
The Vision of
the First Confederation

We are a nation that has lost its sense of history. We don't even understand that we have not always been as we are today, ignorant and confused about our past, uncertain about ourselves, and skeptical about the future. We will regain confidence in ourselves only when we understand what has really happened to us.

We have accepted so many irrelevant versions of our own history. The most pernicious: that we are an accident of history – "a mere accident of history," in the words of André Siegfried, a French writer who wrote a book about Canada in 1947 and who decided that this country had no "centre of gravity – politically it is in England and geographically it is in the United States." Siegfried's analysis and others like it have been embraced by many Canadians in this century. All the most negative judgements about us have stood the test of time. Voltaire's disparaging remark about New France being nothing but a few acres of snow is hardly one of his most sparkling or perceptive but it is the one most widely quoted in Canada. "O God! O Montreal!" groaned the English author Samuel Butler in the nineteenth century, and guaranteed himself a place in every Canadian anthology.

It's been said – and we have cherished this also – that we exist as a nation only because no one important knew what to do with us. By the middle of the nineteenth century, the British no longer wanted us. The United States couldn't prevent itself from making a few aggressive moves in our direction, given its own nature, but Washington really wasn't interested. And so, according to this version of events, Canada drifted into nationhood. We simply filled a vacuum with an artificial political creation that nature and most of us have since found abhorrent.

19

No other nation has fashioned for itself such a history of irrelevance. Only a people who found their true history intolerable could be driven to seek shelter within a history that glorifies their impotence.

It represents, of course, a search for absolution. If we are only an afterthought of history, a by-product of more important national developments beyond our frontiers, then surely we are not accountable for our failures. Even if we are, according to this national apologia, they are hardly worth examining. Why should anyone else pay attention to them if we don't, particularly if the whole experience looks as if it will peter out in the near future?

But this doesn't reflect our real history. It merely shows what we have come to think of ourselves. Every nation makes what it wants of its history. In its imperial heyday, Britain glorified its past; in a more difficult present, it sees a more complex history. Despite their problems, Americans still glorify their fight for independence and celebrate the founding of their nation. There is irony today in visiting the giant statue of Abraham Lincoln in Washington and reading the words carved into the stone walls of his shrine. His dream of brotherhood and justice stands as a reproach to the American people today, but they have not abandoned it. They still learn about it and quote from it.

Beneath the statues of our first great leader, John A. Macdonald, there is almost never anything but his name and not always that in Quebec, where the spray-painters deface it with their slogans. The most eloquent of the founders of our country, Thomas D'Arcy McGee, has a statue on Parliament Hill in Ottawa but only his name appears on it. His words have been obliterated and forgotten so completely it is as if we had set out, Soviet-style, to erase his influence.

Americans embrace and absorb even their most traumatic national experiences. Their destructive civil war in the nineteenth century has become a source of strength. We have been driven to the point of apologizing to history for not having tried to exterminate one another. Because we have escaped serious internal revolution, we have told ourselves, our national development has been irrevocably handicapped.

All these versions of our history falsify the record and belittle the men who devised our first Confederation. Not only did they know what they were doing on a political level but they were inspired by a grand vision of the future. So vast is the difference between them and ourselves that we can hardly bear to look at them as they really were; and they were typical Canadians of their time, filled with a self-confident optimism that makes them seem Olympian in our eyes.

Many of us trace our origin directly from these men. All of us share in their heritage. I remember my own astonishment when I first read correspondence and published writings of my great-grandfather, a printer and publisher at the time of Confederation. Even before there was a Confederation, he was at home in its various parts, living and working in Quebec, Montreal, Kingston, and Ottawa. He launched a daily newspaper in New York, the most competitive market in the world. His writings made it clear that he considered Montreal to be on a level with the greatest American cities. The idea that he was not the equal of an American, or anyone else, would have seemed outlandish to him. He was, I think, typical of his time. The history of our first Confederation is peopled by men like him and it is tumultuous with their self-confident assertions of future greatness.

This rhetoric of nationhood was more than an isolated burst of patriotism triggered by the political excitement of bringing together into a national union British colonies that previously had been independent and competitive. The idea of union had been in the wind for some time as British North Americans began to comprehend the vast territory that lay before them, with its cities and farms in the heartland and, in the distant west, soil that was "beyond example rich and productive."

In the decade before Confederation, more and more Canadians developed a clear image of "the future destiny of that immense tract of country which extends from the Atlantic to in fact the Pacific coast." This was the vision that inspired a Montreal lawyer, Alexander Morris, when he published in 1858 a lecture on "the extent and future of British North America" in which he described the "rapid rise, steady growth, present prosperity and brilliant future of this our country." Our total population at that time was only a few hundred thousand larger than the current population of Toronto or Montreal but Morris boasted about Canada's "rising manufactures, her mineral wealth, her agricultural advantages, her magnificent system of inland navigation, her great railway (the longest in the world), her highway to Europe and her successful ocean line of steamers."

Alexander Morris saw more than railways and canals. He saw a confident people "inheriting, as we do, all the characteristics of the British people, combining with the chivalrous feeling and impulsiveness of France and fusing other nationalities which mingle here with these." He urged a sense of "honest pride" on his compatriots as he described their "noble destiny."

It was a hopeful time for our ancestors who were emerging from a century of economic boom and bust amid political uncertainty. French-speaking Canadians had struggled to overcome the effects of military conquest for a hundred years. The British colonies in North America had been sheared in half by the American Revolution. The weak remnants of the British Empire in the north had been invaded by the armies of the new republic to the south – among the first people to test the strength of a nation that would dominate world politics for the next 150 years. Political differences between English and French in Upper and Lower Canada, and between competing economic regions, had almost paralyzed parliamentary government and had inspired serious violence. The Parliament Building in Montreal had been burned and sacked by an enraged mob.

Out of the ashes of conquest, invasion, and civil disorder arose the determination to build a single nation. The men who set out to do this knew what they were doing on a political level and they were inspired by grand visions of the future. The quarrelsome newspapers of the time reflected this despite their partisan differences. In Halifax, the *Morning Chronicle* foresaw that organizing the provinces into "one vast Confederation" would mean that Canadians "should soon possess all the prestige and command all the respect which our numbers and our position would entitle us." The Montreal *Gazette* asked whether Canadians would "rise to the level of the occasion – to settle now the destiny of this northern country?" In Toronto, the *Globe* saw Confederation as "the assertion of our right to take our place among the nations of the world." The prospect, it said, should make the heart of every Canadian "leap with joy."

Our political leaders shared this excitement and inspiration and expressed it. In Nova Scotia, Joseph Howe rose above centuries of suspicion and hostility between English and French in North America to proclaim that "the distinction of race is the invidious theme upon which alarmists love to dwell." George Brown, the Liberal proprietor of the *Globe* in Toronto, the most powerful newspaper of the day, joined forces with John A. Macdonald of the Conservatives in the great venture. George-Etienne Cartier of Quebec declared that "British and French Canadians alike could appreciate and understand their position relative to each other." They co-existed "like great families beside each other, and contact produced a healthy spirit of emulation."

John A. Macdonald, who would become the first prime minister of the new Confederation, conscious of the internal conflicts that had almost destroyed the United States, believed that he was laying the foundations for a strong central parliament that would make Confederation "one people and one government instead of five people and five governments, with merely a point of authority connecting us to a limited and insufficient extent . . . ." But it was the poet of Confederation, Thomas D'Arcy McGee, who saw "in the not remote distance, one great nationality bound, like the shield of Achilles, by the blue rim of the ocean." "All we have to do," said McGee, "is to lift ourselves to the level of our destinies."

These hardly sound like the words of men who believed they were victims of an historical accident.

Beneath the patriotism, of course, there were other motives, as complicated and often as venal as those involved in the founding of any nation. There was fear of the United States and the realization that Britain could no longer be relied on entirely to defend Canadian interests. There was the old rivalry between Quebec and Ontario, each one jockeying for advantage, Quebec trying desperately to defend itself against the rising power of the English-speaking province. Racial prejudice and religious bigotry were as rife as ever. None of these circumstances was remarkable for the Canadians who created our political union. The unusual and indispensable element was their own sense of historic opportunity and their belief that they were founding not just a nation but one of the greatest nations in the world.

"Never was there such an opportunity as now for the birth of a nation," wrote a contemporary writer. "Nous serons maîtres de nos destinées," proclaimed his compatriot in Quebec. "I do hope there is not one Canadian" said George Brown, "who does not look forward with high hope to the day when these northern countries shall stand out among the nations of the world as one great confederation." Brown's own newspaper noted in the usual parentheses that this speech to a party convention was followed by (Cheers).

The applause soon died away. The idealism and optimism of the nineteenth century were eroded and soured by decades of internal squabbling. We had moved so far from the blithe patriotism of McGee by the 1970's that a group of futurologists in Montreal, commencing a book on our future, felt they had to begin by reminding us that "Canada has not always had a dismal image of its future."

When this nation came into being in 1867, there was a dream of greatness. This generation hardly knows of its existence. We must remember it now to understand how badly we have failed.

3.
An Excuse for History

If we don't often think of Canada as a failure, it's because we don't often think of Canada as a real nation. We prefer to consider its history and its current problems in isolated fragments: the Riel rebellion of the nineteenth century; the military conscription dilemmas of the two world wars; the October Crisis of 1970; the Quebec problem; the Alberta problem. We have become so fragmented we have almost lost the ability to look at ourselves as one people.

Refusing to stand back and look at the whole picture is also a protective device. It is difficult to look at our history since the first Confederation of 1867 without realizing, inescapably, that it is a history of failure. Failure is the unifying theme.

Those who have perceived the failure have tried to balance it against other achievements. No counterbalance is of sufficient weight because our failure is at the fulcrum of our attempt to achieve a stable society. It fractures the central point, the keystone of the structure created by John A. Macdonald and his colleagues more than a century ago. When that point failed to hold, the whole structure became unstable. All our achievements have been contaminated by that failure. We can no longer avoid understanding this in making a herculean effort to renew the structure before it becomes irreparable.

The special challenge confronting Canada has always been the existence of two national communities within this country divided one from the other by history, language, and, to a diminishing extent, religion. For the politicians of Macdonald's time, the problem was to devise a political structure to accommodate both these communities, to bring Canada East and Canada West into the union in a meaningful partnership. Macdonald and his colleagues realized that everything depended on this and everything would flow from it. They also knew

24

how difficult it would be. In one respect, they succeeded more brilliantly than they had initially dared to hope: the final vote in the joint legislature of the two Canadas in favour of the plan of federation was 91 to 33.

As historians have always pointed out, twenty-two of those opposing votes came from Québécois who represented French-speaking constituents of Canada East, but it also was true that there was a new element in the new formula, at least for a short while: a sense of idealism about the country and optimism about its prospects. If Confederation was not the expression of a unified political community, perhaps the unified structure would shape the community. Or so many Canadians hoped.

It was a vain hope. As many newer nations are discovering today, a sense of national unity and purpose is difficult to impose from the top. From the beginning, Canadians failed to live up to the magnificent assumptions of the fathers of Confederation.

There were many reasons. French-speaking Québécois, a century after their abandonment by France, were still recovering from the initial attempts to assimilate them. They were suspicious of change and had only accepted Confederation as the least objectionable of a number of poor options. English-speaking Canadians, in the heyday of the British Empire, were often arrogant and overbearing, impatient of attempts to mollycoddle the native French-Canadians. Religious differences combined with language divisions to create enmities that, to our eyes, seem intractable. There were regional differences between people used to functioning as colonies dependent on London but independent of one another. There were innumerable reasons to explain the failure of the first Confederation and our histories contain them all. Canadian history is, in the main, a string of excuses.

Less than thirty years after the exuberance of Confederation, Wilfrid Laurier, about to become our greatest national leader since Macdonald, had decided that we had "come to a point in the history of this young country where premature dissolution seems to be at hand." Laurier said that his objective was to "bring our people, long estranged from each other, gradually to become a nation." Not only had there been no progress in the decades since Confederation; it was as if the whole premise of Confederation had vanished from living memory.

We all know what happened. All our histories repeat the same story in one form or another. The only point in going over it again briefly is to see it stripped of all the partisan pleading and academic hedging that

25

has confused and protected us in the past. As a substitute for history, we have always had a multitude of histories written from a bewildering variety of viewpoints. Plain history has been too strong for us. We have preferred our history ice-cold with as little emotion as possible. Little wonder that generations of Canadians believed that our history was dull. Lately, in keeping with fashion, we have taken to mixing it with a little artificial carbonation, to persuade ourselves that our story is just as interesting as the fizzy product that Americans use to refresh themselves, but the basic ingredients have been the same.

If our history seemed dull, it was because we couldn't bring ourselves to see what it meant. It was a mystery to us, and not even a good mystery because we wouldn't admit that murder had been committed. We couldn't find the corpse because we were still trying to live in it.

Far from being dull, our history has all the tragedy of Hamlet presented with the unremitting persistence of soap opera: the story of a young country of majestic ancestry that failed to discover its own destiny and conspired to bring about its own destruction. We might be terrified by that story but how could we ever have found it boring?

Of all the early mistakes, the disaster in the Canadian West is always cited as one of the most important: How the West Was Lost. At the time of Confederation, the western prairie was ruled by the fur traders of the Hudson's Bay Company and inhabited by Indians and a few thousand Métis, who were buffalo hunters of mixed Quebec and Indian ancestry who spoke French and worshipped in the Catholic Church. The Métis were a truly Canadian people perhaps capable of bridging the gap between settlers of European origin and the Indians who were being displaced by them. They could hunt with the best of the Indians, and at the same time a young man such as Louis Riel, eventually their leader, was able to absorb the education and culture of central Canada as no Indian could because it was part of his own heritage.

Instead of incorporating and employing the Métis in the settlement of the West, the old protagonists in central Canada used them as pawns. The more powerful of the protaganists tried to exterminate them while the weaker was cast inevitably as their defender. Both roles were predictable and neither was enacted with much dignity. As for the larger national interests that had inspired Macdonald and McGee only a few years earlier, they were forgotten in the struggle.

When the western provinces eventually patterned themselves after Ontario, it was understood that the French of central Canada had lost while the English had won. In fact, we all had lost. The chance to construct a better society in western Canada that was the product of the best aspects of Confederation was thrown away. The West was contaminated at birth by the most poisonous aspects of the old quarrel. This was the heritage central Canada bequeathed to the West, and if the West today is filled with suspicion and hostility toward the old heartland perhaps this is why. Perhaps there is a deep memory of injustice and enmity in the West that has spoiled the "parental" relationship ever since.

With these influences shaping the West, no one should be surprised, least of all central Canada, that it soon displayed some of the worst characteristics of the failure at the centre. The heritage that Quebec and Ontario had given to the West soon rebounded on them with deadly new vigour. During the First World War, as the prospect of military conscription wreaked havoc in the traditional party system in Canada, the country was distracted by a fierce internal struggle over schools and language in Manitoba as well as Ontario. The controversy over schools in Manitoba became so bitter that it infects politics in that province to this day. Sixty-three years ago, it helped to keep Québécois hostile toward the rest of Canada, and at odds with it over military conscription at a time when the war overseas demanded an extraordinary national effort from us. As a result, an experience that unified and inspired English Canada was remembered in French Canada for its divisive effects.

The same experience was repeated in the Second World War when a plebiscite on military conscription was adopted in every part of the country except Quebec. So weak was the national spirit by this time that many of the future leaders of Quebec were among the most prominent objectors to military service. The current Mayor of Montreal made his debut on the political platform as an opponent of conscription just as the Mayor of the day was imprisoned in a concentration camp for taking the same stand. The current Premier of Quebec served overseas as a correspondent with the American armed forces rather than submit to conscription at home. If there is one thing that many Canadians know about the current Prime Minister, it is that he chose not to serve his country almost forty years ago while members of their own families were dying overseas.

After the war, it was often said that the winners had lost and the losers had won. Britain and later the United States found it difficult to adapt to international economic changes while Japan and West Germany flourished, but there were structural reasons for this within each country. It had nothing to do with a weakening of national purpose during the war. Under pressure, both allied nations had been able to summon magnificent efforts from their peoples. In Canada, Prime Minister Mackenzie King spent far more time worrying about internal stability than external security. Even when its very existence was threatened from the outside, Canada, as usual, was at war with itself. That was continued long after hostilities ceased in Europe and Asia, and we lost ground steadily.

It wouldn't be just to many forgotten Canadians to say that failure came easily to this country. There were many throughout the years who fought to realize the dream of Confederation. Particularly tragic was the fate of progressive spirits in Quebec in the nineteenth century – men such as those Liberals who joined the Institut Canadien to attempt to liberate Quebec politics from religious interference. Their writings remind us that there were Canadians who clearly saw other ways for their country to develop. They fought against religious prejudice. Laurier was this kind of Québécois and there were many others who agreed in principle with Macdonald. They agreed with Macdonald that the old conflicts had to be buried, that to speak of any part of Canada as being "a conquered country was *à propos de rien.*" They fought for the freedom of the electoral process, of the schools, of the working man and woman. They tried to join hands across all the old divisions. And they were brushed aside by the majority, excommunicated by their Church in Quebec, given not a single token of success during their lifetimes, and almost forgotten by history.

Perhaps it was even harder in English-speaking Canada where the abuses of authority were not as evident as in Quebec. Progressive spirits in English Canada had to contend not merely with an authoritarian structure of church and government but with a popular consensus that tolerated no criticism. Opponents of the prevailing mood in English Canada were not trampled down by authority, as were the strikers who briefly took over the city of Winnipeg after the First World War, but they suffered the same fate in the end. They were ignored and quickly forgotten. Even today, when we remember the Winnipeg Strike, the early feminists, radicals such as Norman Bethune who abandoned us for more promising peoples in Spain and China, we tend to recall them in isolated fragments – a book here, a television documentary there. They don't bother us because we see them as curiosities, not as part of a pattern.

These were men and women who wanted to free Canadians from the divisions of the past, who believed that this country could change. They fought against the mainstream of opinion and were overwhelmed by it. They did not understand that Canadians cherished the divisions of the past and that change was anathema. We did not want to be free, and, if necessary, we would imprison those who tried to free us.

This is the truth about ourselves. For a moment, at the time of Confederation, we glimpsed another kind of existence. We defined it for ourselves. We even gave ourselves the laws and political structure within which it could have happened. But we weren't up to it.

They say that we are a dull people, unemotional. That is perhaps the most grotesque of all the myths that we perpetuate about ourselves. The dullness is on the surface. At heart, we literally seethe with a fierce mixture of passions.

The most characteristic Canadian passion, and the only one that joins us from coast to coast, is hatred.

There are many kinds of hatred. There is the mild dislike of people who come from another region, particularly if they represent a threat to one's own security or prosperity. There is the distrust that always exists between one class and another, between the top and the bottom of the system. There is the fear of someone who practises a different religion or speaks a language both impenetrable and ominous. All these hatreds exist within our country, as they do everywhere else in the world, but they come together with special force in Canada. If there is a spirit that has shaped our country since Confederation it is the combined influence of all these hatreds expressed ultimately in the continuing struggle between Canadians who speak English and Canadians who speak French, between Quebec and the rest of Canada.

The highest purpose of the first Confederation was to overcome that spirit of hatred and to replace it with mutual respect and co-operation. No one can pretend that we have achieved this. On the contrary, we have failed every test, and each failure has made the next attempt more difficult. As the original purpose of Confederation has become increasingly unattainable, our rage and our frustration with one another has grown.

This is extreme, you say? For the past twenty years, I have listened to us. Sometimes I feel that I've spent a lifetime taking notes in various commissions of inquiry in every part of the country, listening to Canadians trying to comprehend their problems in communications, industrial development, labour relations, internal security, air traffic safety, bilingualism, constitutional reform, and on and on. The same themes are repeated over and over – hostility toward one another, suspicion, resentment, every form in which hatred manifests itself.

My work as a journalist and commentator also has opened me to individual contacts with a wide range of people. I have sat at John Diefenbaker's breakfast table and felt myself pinioned by his preconceptions about the attitudes of anyone from Quebec. I have squinted against the glare of Pierre Trudeau's dazzling blindness about western Canada – an emotional handicap masquerading as political logic. More impressive than these because more pervasive have been the letters, telephone calls, and street-corner communications with thousands of Canadians over the years. I'm thinking about all the anonymous calls and letters accusing me of being anti-French, anti-English, anti-Catholic, anti-Protestant, anti-Trudeau, anti-Diefenbaker . . . a constant communication from the depths of the Canadian subconscious. Any public figure who expresses an opinion in this country soon hears from this lower strata of the silent majority. Eventually you realize it is always there, generation after generation, eternal and implacable, like the permafrost under so much of the Canadian surface.

Another kind of communication is even more disturbing because it is often personable and intelligent: the callers identify themselves; the letters are signed; professions of understanding and toleration are presented; some of their best friends are cited to illustrate their own innocence. When the preamble is over, the main message is virtually the same as those from the anonymous neanderthals. It is always arrived at reluctantly. There is always simply no other response to circumstances. It is never anyone's fault. This is closer to the face we present to the world. I have decided, after years of exposure to it, that it is simply a toilet-trained version of the anonymous primitive.

After years of such "open-line" communication with public opinion in our country, anyone would lose the illusion that we are a dispassionate and inherently tolerant people. We are in a constant state of suppressed fury with one another. But we have suppressed it, except for rare outbursts in our history. We have become more and more adept at concealing it.

In the nineteenth century, in addition to expressing our idealism about our country, we were also more honest about stating our hatred of one another. Newspapers were filled with crude cartoons about "frogs" swarming over the countryside, the English defecating on Quebec, and the clergy growing fat on the tithes of the poor and the favour of politicians. English and French hurled rocks at one another in the streets of our major cities. Songs of defiance were roared at one another on public holidays. Almost all of this has now been brought under control. The mask is firmly in place. It has been accepted as the real face.

This is finally threatening to destroy us. It has made our most serious internal divisions almost invisible to us. Losing the ability to perceive our failures clearly is taking us a long way toward losing our ability to learn from them. Losing sight of the real past is causing us to lose control of our future. We are in the process of abdicating control over our own lives. The symptoms are everywhere.

4.
The Failure of
Canadian Democracy

The first Confederation would have been successful if Canadians had been able to overcome their past failures and to deal with one another in a spirit of freedom and equality. The prospect of a great adventure in democracy lay before us but we turned away from it. We were unwilling to accept the risks involved in confronting our differences, changing our society, and taking control of our national destiny.

The risks might have been considerable. There might have been serious, internal disturbances, perhaps even civil war. Instability in the new Confederation might have forced Britain to place us under some new form of tutelage. The United States might have been forced or invited to intervene to maintain the security of the continent.

The rewards are easier to imagine. Without the constant infection of internal discord, we would have become one of the wonders of this century. The material expansion that sprang from the original enthusiasm of Confederation, even with all its flaws, would have continued, perhaps bringing us earlier into an age of resource wealth and northward development. Settlement of new territories would have been nourished by both older sources of population in central Canada, as well as by new arrivals who would soon have been accommodated in this integrated society. The "Quebec problem," if it continued to exist at all, would have been a national problem of equal concern to all of us.

One thing is certain: we would have been a far more democratic society than we are today, more confident of our ability to handle our own affairs. That would have had a profound effect on our economic development and our political institutions. We would have valued the freedom to be ourselves. We could have explored the limits of democratic society. The best thoughts of Macdonald, Cartier, and McGee would still have meant something to us.

We drew back from this prospect because we couldn't overcome our own fear, distrust, and dislike of one another. That failure to grasp our own destiny then dictated the shape of the future. We can see that failure in what we have become.

It's been said that we are the most upper-middle-class country in the world; that description is partly a tribute to the prosperity that we have achieved and to the comfortable existence that we have bought for ourselves. Our cities are clean and secure, often surrounded by the farms and forests of controlled greenbelts. Many of our schools and universities are luxurious. New cultural centres have opened their doors in the past few decades in every major city. We have one of the most elaborate social welfare systems outside of Scandinavia. Health insurance protects all of us and most working Canadians contribute to a government pension plan.

Like all upper-middle-class people, we like our comforts; we like an orderly world. Anyone who can provide this for us has our allegiance.

Democracy is one of the few luxuries that we often can do without. In politics, we tend to be a rather bovine herd. Placid in appearance, we chew the bitter cud of old disappointments and current frustrations while the managers of our society provide for us, and managing our society has become one of our most popular and rewarding careers. It has often been said that we are the most over-governed society in the Western world.

Our closest standard of comparison is the United States. It is estimated that 32 per cent of the gross national product of the United States is consumed in one form or another by federal, state, or local governments. That degree of government activity has been enough to create a conservative American reaction against big government. The same reaction is noticeable in Canada but in milder form, despite the fact that government spending in this country accounts for an estimated 43 per cent of our gross national product. This means that 43 cents of every dollar earned by Canadians goes to the government rather than remaining in our own hands to spend, save, or invest, and the trend has been sharply in favour of the government. In 1964, only 30 cents of every dollar of national income went to the government.

Big government is usually associated in our minds with the federal government in Ottawa. In the past decade, the federal budget has increased five-fold in current dollars. Most of these billions are recycled by government and returned to us in one form or another but only after they have passed through the hands of an army of civil servants. No one seems to know exactly how many Canadians are on the public payroll. Even this simple sum is confused and obscured by the bureaucracy. About 280,000 people work directly for the federal government under its Public Service Commission, but these represent little more than half of the total Canadian bureaucracy.

The official estimates of government spending presented to Parliament every year now provide for about 330,000 employees, including the Royal Canadian Mounted Police and the staff of the Canadian Broadcasting Corporation. When the armed forces and employees of Crown corporations are added, the federal payroll lengthens to include about half a million people. Another 2,000,000 Canadians work for provincial and municipal governments. All told, one out of every ten Canadians works for the government, if the size of the bureaucracy is compared with the national population. By comparing it with the labour force, some experts have estimated that 23 per cent of all Canadians at work in the 1970's were working for the government. We all have to work hard just to meet this massive payroll. The total tax bite from our incomes is estimated to be 33 per cent. Even at the height of the Second World War, it never rose higher than 27 per cent.

Government in Ottawa has come a long way in the past century from the days when our second Prime Minister, Alexander Mackenzie, answered his own mail without the help of a private secretary. Prime Minister Trudeau now has a staff of more than a hundred. This "personal" staff is matched in the bureaucracy by the staff of the Privy Council Office headed by the Clerk of the Privy Council, Michael Pitfield, the "prime minister" of the bureaucracy. It employs about four hundred people. The combined operations of the Prime Minister's Office and the Privy Council Office cost the taxpayers more than $22 million a year.

In 1965, the government telephone directory in Ottawa contained 200 pages. Ten years later, the listings in French and English had expanded to fill 818 pages. The number of people working for the federal government increased by an estimated 44 per cent during that decade.

In addition to its own departments, the federal government owns or controls 380 corporations with total assets of $30 billion. A survey of 27 of these Crown corporations a few years ago by the government's own Auditor-General showed that they had required $700 million of public funds to offset operating losses.

At the top of this huge structure is a bureaucratic elite whose power, stability, and affluence surpass the ambitions of the fabled bureaucracies of the old Chinese empires. Canada's own "mandarins" now virtually run the country, according to the testimony of the politicians who are supposed to be their masters.

As the public service increased in size in the past few decades, it mushroomed at the top. Between 1969 and 1975, the number of federal public servants earning $20,000 a year or more went from 1,225 to 16,868. Salaries at the top level now exceed $85,000 a year. Cutbacks in the public service in the past few years have had little effect either on the salaries or size of the bureaucratic elite. While the number of federal civil servants declined by 7,883 in the austerity year of 1979, only 18 senior executives were laid off, and the creation of new executive positions at the same time meant that the number of senior executives actually increased by 18.

This expansion of the number of civil service managers of our affairs has not produced better management. Exactly the opposite, according to a series of studies of government efficiency, many of them conducted by the bureaucrats themselves. Former Auditor-General J.J. McDonnell, the "watchdog" of government spending who retired in 1980, said many times in recent years that federal spending was literally "out of control." McDonnell spent his years in Ottawa fighting for a system to ensure that taxpayers received value for money spent. Many bureaucrats regarded that as a radical and dangerous departure.

A bureaucratic committee that studied personnel management in the federal civil service from 1977 to 1979 stated, in the D'Avignon Report, that there was no philosophy of management and no way to make personnel managers accountable for inefficiencies. The same problem of accountability was the chief concern of a commission of expert outsiders that investigated financial management in the public service from 1976 to 1979. The Lambert Commission found that there was a "serious malaise" in government service and that it stemmed from "a grave weakening, and in some cases an almost total breakdown, in the chain of accountability." Civil servants were not accountable to their superiors, according to the Lambert Commission, and their superiors were not accountable to politicians. "We have a wallowing monster," admitted one bureaucrat to newspaper columnist Douglas Fisher.

The same irresponsibility pervades the provincial bureaucracies that have grown at an even faster rate in recent decades. An unpublished draft memorandum to the Ontario cabinet in 1979 quoted an anonymous civil servant as saying, "Mine not to reason why; mine but to beat the other son-of-a-bitch without being caught breaking the rules."

Stories about the size and cost of the civil service, the luxurious offices of deputy ministers in Ottawa, their indexed pensions to keep them ahead of inflation after retirement, and the protection and even encouragement of inefficiency at senior levels have inundated the Canadian public for decades. They are only the superficial, spectacular signs of a breakdown in the system. They occur year after year because we literally have lost control of our own affairs. This can be clearly seen at those points in Ottawa where the politicians and the bureaucrats meet and where our ability to shape our own destiny should be most evident.

Many politicians have testified to this breakdown. One of the most eloquent is an anonymous Member of Parliament who talked with the academic authors of *The Super-Bureaucrats*, a study of the "Structure and behaviour of central agencies" in Ottawa published in 1979. This young MP several years ago was picked from the backbenches in the House of Commons to serve as parliamentary secretary to the President of the Treasury Board, the federal minister who controls government spending and who is among the most powerful in the cabinet. A first appointment such as that is crucial for an ambitious politician and this one took his job seriously. He introduced himself to the senior bureaucracy of the Treasury Board and started to learn something about their operations. Soon he decided it would be useful for him to attend the regular Monday morning senior staff meeting chaired by the secretary of the Board, its top civil servant. When he suggested this, he was told by the bureaucrats that it was out of the question. He took the issue to his minister and the bureaucratic decision prevailed.

This episode expresses the problem in Ottawa more dramatically than all the newspaper headlines about government mismanagement. The public business cannot be entrusted to politicians, the bureaucrats decided. The inner sanctums of real power in Ottawa cannot be violated by a mere Member of Parliament.

Many politicians have now testified publicly to this distortion of our democracy. Former Conservative Leader Robert Stanfield has stated bluntly that "we no longer have parliamentary responsible government in Ottawa," that the House of Commons "cannot control the government." A researcher who interviewed seventy-five Members of Parliament in 1972 found that they suffered from a "vague, generalized sense of discontent." Dissatisfaction was highest, not surprisingly, among the youngest, brightest, and most ambitious, some of whom later dropped out of the system.

Understanding the actual power structure in Ottawa is difficult because government in Canada is one of the most secretive among the Western democracies. Most of the government decisions that affect us are made not in the open forum of Parliament but behind the closed doors of the cabinet, which issues about 3,000 orders-in-council a year under the guidance of the bureaucrats. Power in Canada is exercised in well-guarded privacy by a small number of people whose identity, in many cases, remains hidden from most of us. A majority of bureaucrats surveyed for *The Super-Bureaucrats* maintained that really important decisions in Ottawa are made by an "inner circle" of ministers and senior bureaucrats. Recently there's been reason to ask whether even this limited and secretive political input is effective. As the study of government becomes more developed in our country, and Ottawa structures are probed more thoroughly than before, the proposition that this country is administered exclusively by and for bureaucrats has become more tenable.

Everyone in Ottawa has stories that illustrate this. My own most recent glimpse of bureaucratic power was provided by Michel Choquette, a Montreal writer and satirist who by chance became interested some years ago in the case of an elderly Hungarian-Canadian milk powder exporter. David Schafer's complaint of unfair treatment by the Canadian Dairy Commission is now being heard by a special federal inquiry, but if the usual Canadian practice had been followed, it would have been buried in the files of the Ottawa bureaucracy years ago.

The export of skim milk powder and many other agricultural products is a highly technical business and so of little public interest, despite the huge amounts of money involved and the temptations of cosy relationships, among politicians, bureaucrats, state marketing agencies, and private enterprise. Unable to attract media interest in the case, Michel Choquette did battle on Schafer's behalf directly with the bureaucracy. For several years nothing happened as bureaucrats appointed bureaucrats to investigate other bureaucrats. The process was time-consuming, costly for Choquette and Schafer, and led nowhere. Even the active interest of Schafer's MP and a former Consumer Affairs Minister, Warren Allmand, did nothing to budge the bureaucracy.

The only factor that made a difference was Michel Choquette's personal and long-standing friendship with Prime Minister Trudeau. That finally broke through the stonewalling of the bureaucracy and resulted in the appointment of the official inquiry at the last meeting of the Trudeau cabinet before the election of 1979. Choquette had managed to get the documentation about the case directly into the Prime Minister's hands and to convince him that the affair warranted a special inquiry. Trudeau overrode the bureaucracy and Schafer is being given his day in court, but how often does the average citizen happen to find an eccentric scuba-diving companion of the Prime Minister's to represent his interests with an almost fanatic tenacity?

The Prime Minister's effective authority over the bureaucracy may be questionable. In theory he has immense power within our parliamentary system compared, for example, with the U.S. President. In practice, the Prime Minister suffers from the disabilities that hamper all politicians in our system in competition with the bureaucracy. He is only one man with limited time at his disposal while they are legion and eternal. Even such a leader as Pierre Trudeau may be the prime victim of the bureaucracy rather than its master. Studies of his first terms in office have shown that Trudeau was unable to enlist enough support within the bureaucracy for his early promises to establish a "just society" by reducing unemployment and lessening the income gap between rich and poor. State and business bureaucracies were more influenced by fears of inflation than the Prime Minister's campaign commitments and policy objectives.

The Financial Post recently quoted a senior civil servant in Ottawa as saying, "People who really want to guide and influence government policy are wasting their time dealing with MPs, Senators and, usually, even ministers. If you want results, you deal with us." Andrew Roman, executive director of The Public Interest Advocacy Centre in Ottawa, has summed up the secret of influence-peddling in the capital: "If you can persuade Pitfield or Coutts, that's the end of the matter. If you can't, don't bother trying lower."

The inclusion here of Jim Coutts, Principal Secretary to the Prime Minister and head of his political staff, perhaps indicates some lingering political influence over the mandarins, even if it is exercised by a backroom political figure rather than by an elected politician. This linking of the top bureaucrat and the chief party worker also shows how blurred the distinction between bureaucrat and policy-maker has become. Pitfield himself personifies this confusion. A personal friend of the Prime Minister's, he had become so closely identified with Pierre Trudeau over the years that the fall of the Liberal government in 1979 forced him to step aside, much against his will. It was politically impossible for the Conservative government to retain him. As soon as Trudeau returned to power in 1980, Pitfield returned to his old job.

The traditional separation of bureaucrat and politician has lessened under Pitfield, who is "ambivalent about the dichotomy between politics and bureaucracy," according to a senior bureaucrat quoted in *The Super-Bureaucrats*. "Pitfield tends to get involved," he said. "If things get screwed up politically, he will say, 'Damn, we should have avoided that!' "

If the true influence of the bureaucracy is hidden from most Canadians, it has certainly been identified by those who seek favours in Ottawa. A survey of interest groups in Canada and the United States showed that legislators rather than bureaucrats in the United States were the prime target for lobbyists by a margin of two-to-one. In Canada, the ratio was exactly reversed: bureaucrats were sought over politicians. Perhaps this has something to do with the nature of the bureaucracy here. In the United States, about one-third of all positions in the senior echelons of the federal bureaucracy are filled by presidential appointments or non-career executive assignments. The Canadian bureaucracy is staffed almost exclusively by career civil servants.

Attempts have been made in Ottawa to bring outside executive talent into the bureaucracy for short periods, as the Americans do, but without much success. Tradition and the resistance of the bureaucracy to outside influences work against it. In days of rampant patronage, this resistance of the bureaucracy was one of its strengths and helped to keep it independent of politics. Bureaucrats in those days were generally underpaid, conservative by nature, and, at the upper levels, often idealistic. Now there is no longer any danger of bureaucracies changing with governments. Civil service jobs are secure under all but the worst economic conditions. The problem is the reverse; to make the bureaucracy at least somewhat responsive to pressure for changes in political policies.

The obduracy of the bureaucracy has become such a feature of our political life that we now almost take it for granted that when governments change in Ottawa it will mean little change in policy. When Prime Minister Trudeau was voted out of office in 1979, one authority estimated that it would take the new Conservative government at least one full term of four years to re-orient the bureaucracy. In that instance, it was saved from this heroic effort by the return of the Liberals early in 1980.

Shortly after that event, one of the most important of the Conservatives' former ministers testified to the influence of the bureaucracy in a remarkably candid speech to a group of political scientists. Her term in office as External Affairs Minister had led Flora MacDonald to conclude that in Ottawa "the Minister is indeed at the mercy of bureau-cratic domination, not because of some devious manipulative plot, but simply because that's the way the system has been allowed to develop." MacDonald quoted former U.S. Secretary of State Henry Kissinger with approval when she said that even the most dedicated bureaucrats possessed the conviction that "a lifetime of service and study has given them insights that transcend the untrained and shallow-rooted views of political appointees." She was particularly critical of senior mandarins, saying that they seemed to resist creativity and imagination coming from lower ranks of the civil service as vigorously as they resisted out-side advice.

MacDonald outlined a variety of tactics used by senior bureaucrats against ministers – jolting the ministers continually with "unnecessarily numerous crisis corridor decisions," inundating them with long memos, delaying important documents until the last minute so that few changes could be made before they were adopted as policy – which in total seemed to amount to a deliberate strategy to manipulate the elected politician. She discovered that secret cabinet documents were somehow finding their way into her deputy minister's hands without her knowledge, giving this bureaucrat privileged information not possessed by some members of the cabinet.

As MacDonald told her academic audience, the problem is not unique in Canada. She referred to a lecture by Anthony Wedgewood Benn, in which the former British cabinet minister said that the civil service "sees itself as being above the party battle, with a political posi-tion of its own to defend." Benn referred to "civil service policy" as an identifiable force usually in conflict with new political ideas. Mac-Donald suspected that this tendency is "even more entrenched" in Canada because of the long domination of the Liberal Party in Ottawa. It is, but for more fundamental reasons.

The British at least are working within their own tradition. We aren't. While we have adapted much of Britain's constitutional and administrative tradition to our own purposes over the past few cen-turies, much has remained irrelevant to the problems of Canadian federalism. There are many places where our theory of government and the reality of our politics don't jibe, as our own basic ideas about our country often fail to reflect what actually happens in Canada. Ameri-can authorities look at their own bureaucracy and see that "American values shape the bureaucratic structure." In Canada, bureaucratic values now attempt to shape our national structure. This is at the heart of our parliamentary malaise and at the centre of many of our national problems.

How tragic it is, for example, that our national decision in favour of bilingualism in the 1960's should have been expressed as a battle within the federal bureaucracy. This alone says a great deal about us. It was inevitable that the reform would be seen in terms of bureaucratic rather than popular change just as it was predetermined that the bureaucrats would resist change, would complicate it, would make it terribly expensive, and would almost succeed in discrediting the whole attempt. Finally, they have made it impossible to determine whether this expensive controversy achieved anything. Year after year, the Commissioner of Official Languages tries and fails to discover from his fellow bureaucrats the number of their colleagues in various government departments who have been trained to speak a second language and who actually use it at work. Reams of statistics spew out of government computers every day in Ottawa, but not this one, and it is, of course, the only one that matters.

Bureaucrats working for provincial governments and educational institutions also have frustrated the intent of the language reform symbolized by parliamentary approval of the Official Languages Act in 1969. Because French or English as a second language is optional in most schools, the number of high school students taking French has dropped precipitously from 55 per cent in 1970 to 41 per cent in 1979. This has occurred while the federal government spends $38 million a year on bilingual bonuses for civil servants, a system so fraught with inefficiencies that the Commissioner of Official Languages estimates that at least half of this money is "misplaced and embarrassing."

Where the hand of the bureaucrat is absent, the real desires of Canadians make themselves felt. At the local level, in elementary schools in eight provinces (Quebec and Alberta were not included in this survey) the number of English-speaking students in French "immersion" classes increased by 32 per cent from 1976 to 1978. The desire to have English-speaking children educated in French was so strong in certain school districts that it was difficult to maintain enough students in the traditional English-language system. This was the case in my own district in Ottawa where many federal bureaucrats were demanding an opportunity for their own children that the bureaucracy as a whole seemed determined to oppose.

More than ten years after the Official Languages Act was passed, our snail's-pace progress toward bilingualism in this country reveals the power of the bureaucracy to distort and oppose the national will, even when it is clearly stated by our political leaders.

We have reached the point where often we despair of making changes before we have even tried because we anticipate the opposition of the bureaucracies. For years, Canadian politicians have suggested replacing our costly and cumbersome system of social welfare payments by using our tax system to provide the poorest among us with a guaranteed annual income. The main objection to this scheme, among several listed this year by G. Bruce Doern, Director of the School of Public Administration at Ottawa's Carleton University, was that "such a tax-based scheme reduces the size of the federal and provincial bureaucracy."

If bureaucrats can oppose political changes, it stands to reason that they can initiate them. There was a curious example of this from 1977 to 1979 when the Minister of Transport had legislation before Parliament to reorganize the bureaucracy of the Canadian port system. According to an Ottawa transportation consultant, Wilbrod Leclerc, writing in *The Financial Post*, the changes in the National Harbours Board were bureaucratic in inspiration. They were not based on requests from the public or the shipping trade. A report to the Canadian Transport Commission in 1978, before the legislation had been passed by Parliament, revealed that the proposed change "has been largely implemented already. . . . most positions have been filled and the essential groupings accomplished." It was estimated that this bureaucratic reorganization already had cost more than $5 million.

Among the most flagrant recent examples of government by the bureaucracy have been those provided by our security agencies to the McDonald Inquiry. The inquiry, which has been dragging on since the summer of 1977, has itself been attacked as a bureaucratic effort to delay the prosecution of members of the Royal Canadian Mounted Police and other police forces for illegal activities. Regardless of this, it has provided Canadians with a constant series of revelations about the police which should have shocked us. We discovered that the RCMP has been engaged in opening our mail, arson, theft, illegal surveillance of an official political party which was soon to form the government of Quebec, providing misleading information to the federal cabinet and Parliament, and various other criminal activities. This is the only country in the world, as it has been said, where the policeman has become something of a national symbol. The shock of discovering corruption

42

beneath the red jackets of the Mounties should have been traumatic for Canadians.

In the United States, public and political indignation over a third-rate burglary of a party headquarters was so intense that it drove a president from office. The raiding of a party office by the police in Canada and the theft of party membership lists caused hardly a ripple of excitement when it was revealed. There have been no political repercussions.

Even when illegal police acts touched Canadians directly, there was no national sense of outrage. In a rare example of good investigative reporting, the Canadian Broadcasting Corporation revealed in 1977 that the RCMP had been opening and copying first-class mail under a program entitled "Operation Cathedral." Solicitor-General Francis Fox's first response was to condemn the CBC reporting as "irresponsible" and to suggest that its budget should be cut. He seemed to be worried about the public's reaction to the story. If he was, his political judgement was as faulty as his moral position. Canadians were not alarmed.

The ruling principle was stated for all Canadians by Prime Minister Trudeau at a press conference in 1977. "The minister of the day," he said, "should not have a right to know what the police are doing instantly in their investigative practices." As usual, the Prime Minister tried to discredit his critics by exaggerating their argument. At another press conference in 1977, he confused the issue by muddling two different functions of a cabinet minister – receiving information and issuing instructions. To know what the RCMP was doing, argued the Prime Minister, would open politicians to charges of political influence and interference with the police. When the Prime Minister proclaims that the police should have a free hand, and when the statement does him no harm at all politically, it has to be assumed that he speaks for the people.

Someone has called us a "pleasantly authoritarian country." Only once, in this generation, has the polite mask dropped momentarily to reveal the stern face of authority, during the October Crisis of 1970. Apparently convinced that it faced serious internal disorder, the Trudeau government resurrected the War Measures Act to give itself dictatorial powers. Although no evidence of immediate danger was submitted to Canadians, then or since, Parliament went along with the government and, in the words of historian A.R.M. Lower, "committed suicide."

Ten years later, now that everyone has had second thoughts, that parliamentary majority has evaporated. The New Democratic Party and its leader, T.C. Douglas, showed unusual courage at the time in opposing the Act. "Using a sledge-hammer to crack a peanut" was Douglas's verdict. Since then, Robert Stanfield, who supported the government in 1970 as leader of the Conservative opposition, has changed his mind and now says that he should have voted against it.

The 190-16 vote in the House of Commons reflected overwhelming public approval of the government's tough response to the terrorists. A Gallup poll published several months after the Act came into force showed that 87 per cent of Canadians supported the move, with French-speaking Quebecers as strongly in favour of it as Canadians in other provinces.

Some of us were affected directly by the Act as well as by the atmosphere of crisis. One of the researchers working with me on a public affairs program for the Canadian Broadcasting Corporation in Montreal was summoned by the RCMP from a noon-hour conference and spent several weeks in jail. There was nothing anyone could do for him. Under the provisions of the Act, he had no right to a lawyer or to a hearing of charges against him, had there been any.

Within the CBC, there were official attempts to limit discussion of the crisis on the air. It was claimed later that the same restrictive panic affected Canadian Press, the national co-operative news service that supplies most Canadian newspapers and radio and television stations. Some stories reportedly were cleared through security officials by Canadian Press before they were released, as if the country were in a wartime condition.

Public approval of these measures was not an aberration under pressure. It was in the Canadian tradition.

Even under normal conditions, this most orderly of countries acts as if violence and disorder might disrupt it at any moment. The bureaucracy of internal security is massive and well-paid. The number of police in Canada grew from 32,000 in 1965 to 50,000 in 1975. The pay of a first-class constable tripled during this decade. The RCMP almost doubled in size, from 10,000 to 19,000 men and women, while its budget increased from $75.9 million to $627.5 million.

This army of police helps to maintain the federal prison population at a level of about 9,000 inmates, claimed to be the highest federal prison population in relation to national population of any Western democracy. This has to be qualified because, for example, it doesn't take into account the number of inmates in state prisons in the United States or in provincial jails here, but Canada's prison population is high by any comparison. So is the cost of maintaining this system. There is approximately one guard or other staff member of the penitentiary service for every prisoner. Annual salaries of guards, with overtime for riots and other crisis situations, have been known to reach $30,000.

The system, which costs the taxpayer about $17,000 a year per inmate, fails in every respect. According to a 1977 parliamentary report, our prisons do not fulfil their two essential purposes, "correcting the offender and providing permanent protection to society . . . the recidivist rate of up to 80 per cent is evidence of failure on both counts."

In the sixties, there was a period of public concern about prison conditions in Canada and the lack of rehabilitation efforts within prisons. In the seventies, federal authorities discovered parole as a way to reduce prison costs while satisfying the "liberal" critics of the system. The predictable result was an increase in crime. Public reaction to this also was predictable and swift. Parole was tightened up, new prisons were planned, and even less attention was paid to rehabilitation.

If we cared to look, we could see ourselves reflected in this despairing prison multitude and its caretakers. Like all of us, the prisoners have lost touch with reality and most of them are doomed to make the same mistakes over and over again. The bureaucracy that arrests them, convicts them, and guards them also has lost all sense of purpose or belief in change. It, too, wants only to be left to pursue its own interests. Everyone has become a captive of the past, a victim of previous failures.

All of us are now starting to ask, as if we were prisoners, "Why are we here?" And like prison inmates we produce a variety of reasons to explain our loss of freedom, most of them bogus.

The most comforting explanation is the genetic one, comforting because we can't possibly do anything about it. We've been told that we come from timid stock. Our French-speaking ancestors missed out on the French Revolution while our British ancestors did everything they could to avoid the American one, fleeing from the excesses of democracy to the familiar order and stability of British North America. This is simply another example of how we degrade the past to suit the present. New France beckoned the most adventurous souls from Europe. They explored North America from the Gulf of Mexico to the Pacific. Not all our British ancestors came here by way of the United States, but those who did had their own ideas of freedom which were incompatible with the orthodoxy of the new American Republic. They were also colonizers who had kept their zest for new frontiers while living in the settled and gentler communities of the United States.

These ancestors of modern Canadians would repudiate our attempts to blame them for our failures, as would the immigrants who followed them. In the second half of the nineteenth century, we attracted the same mixture of peoples as did the United States. Our eastern cities harboured the same Irish and Jewish ghettos, displaced in this century by Italians, Portuguese, and West Indians. Our western plains were populated by the same stock – Ukrainians, Germans, Poles, Russians. In the United States, these new arrivals came with a thirst for freedom and drank quickly and deeply at the springs of American democracy. They were proud to be Americans. Here, freedom turned out to be a mirage. In the face of a confusing present and uncertain future, they learned not to abandon their pasts too quickly.

Out of this necessary compromise, we've tried to make a positive virtue. Not for us the American melting pot. We've used the word "mosaic" to describe our dream of a structure of interlocking cultures: a usable technique, perhaps, if we had ever had a pattern for it. But we've fooled no one. Our ethnic groups have remained skeptical of the grand design. For the most part, they have stood outside the main arena of Canadian political development, courted by one side or the other, their votes sought at election time, their voices otherwise ignored, particularly in the periodic bargaining sessions between the two main national communities, between Quebec and Canada, that have determined our development as a nation.

Life has been comfortable for these immigrants and their children, as it has been for all of us. They have lacked only a sense of national identity and purpose. They have never truly belonged because there has been nothing to claim their allegiance. They have been relegated to the role of spectators at a national quarrel that none of them understand, urged to cheer for one side or another. How hard it must have been for many of them, proud peoples eager to love this country passionately. We have told them that their ardour is misplaced; it is un-Canadian.

Citizens of a divided country soon learn to fear patriotism. The emotions that unite other peoples can destroy us, so we have repressed them. We have taught newcomers that Canada is a vast, cold, and unsettled landscape dotted with the fires of various national communities which we should tend carefully lest total darkness overwhelm us.

We must be utterly incomprehensible to many of them, grateful as they may be at times for the peace and quiet we impose on ourselves. We seem to be a nation "queenly and pristine," as a recent arrival from the United States wrote, difficult to know and to love. If only they could understand what we are like inside, the fears and rages that divide us, the hatreds that inspire us. . . .

Edgar Friedenberg, an American immigrant who has written about our *Deference to Authority*, the title of his recent book, has discovered that "more powerful Canadians don't like such questions to be raised . . . and less powerful Canadians find confrontation with their adversaries embarrassing and frightening rather than invigorating." At the close of his book, Friedenberg wrote that "Canadians don't spend as much time and effort fighting one another as Americans do, so they don't get in each other's way as much; they don't waste as much energy on anger and litigation, so they can get more done in a quiet way."

After ten years with us, Friedenberg has absorbed some of our own complacency. As an American "schooled the hard way in the costs and the sometimes devious ways of liberty," he says that he can "afford to enjoy Canada." Still, he wonders if Canadians "may find this indulgence too expensive," and he suggests that "there is a connection between freedom and victory – even between freedom and combat readiness – which might well receive more emphasis than Canadians have traditionally recognized."

How gently put. Friedenberg has learned about our sensitivities if not our secret motivations. An American who comes here soon discovers that one of our most effective weapons against the threat of democracy, equality, and liberty is to describe them as "American." We have been doing this for so long we have lost the ability to see these virtues as valuable in themselves. Certainly we would reject any American guidance in helping us to attain them.

We are nothing if not fastidious in our approach to democracy, pretending to select only the best parts from the British and American models. We are great connoisseurs and critics. We taste expertly but we rarely imbibe. In practice, we are careless about the most basic rights and tolerate the most flagrant abuses of power and privilege. Once again, there is a gap between what we believe ourselves to be and what we really are, and once again, this inconsistency scarcely seems to bother us.

A Gallup survey for the Ontario government in 1980 showed that 63 per cent of those polled mistakenly believed that Canadian police are required to read suspects their legal rights before arresting them. More than 78 per cent of those interviewed believed that anyone arrested in Canada is entitled to a phone call. A majority of those polled also believed that police in this country need a search warrant to search a home or car. Presumably these rights have been imprinted on Canadians by American television. If so, the impression is superficial. The absence of these and other rights in Canada has never been cause for widespread concern.

Our politicians long ago learned that public indignation is a feeble and temporary effect sometimes generated by the news media and often confined to it. They can do almost anything they want with impunity: transport a domestic servant on government aircraft, telephone a judge about a case involving a cabinet minister, or forge a signature on a hospital document authorizing an abortion. Canadians have become accustomed to a series of such revelations in recent years. The guilty politicians usually succeed in persuading themselves and most of us that they are victims of an ill-tempered press brefore returning to their careers, sometimes after a brief retirement from the limelight.

Moral outrage in public affairs doesn't exist in Canada except as a hackneyed device in political speeches, and this is accepted as a conventional exercise in futility by everyone. We have taken the spirit out of our most important dealings with one another and that has taken the heart out of us for contestation. When our two founding societies a century ago turned their backs on freedom and equality and refused to be themselves, to admit their traditional hatreds, when they abandoned the revolution of the first Confederation almost at the outset, we suffered a crippling loss of faith in ourselves.

The damage was emotional. Our instinctive reaction is to dismiss this loss of faith as trivial but our analogies speak louder than our public attitudes. Marriage is the most persistent of our illustrations to describe the union of French and English in this country. We often speak about Confederation as a "shotgun marriage." The separation of Quebec is often thought of as a divorce. We've speculated endlessly about the terms of settlement. We sense that we are like the couple whose passion evaporates soon after the wedding and who choose – for reasons of necessity, duty, or idealism – to stick together. Within a few years, that couple may not perceive or admit the flaw in their union. The longer it endures, the colder become the family relations, the hotter grows the core of anger that finally becomes the dominant theme of the marriage.

Such a marriage in its unrelieved monotony contaminates each partner with a feeling of hopelessness. They are no longer in control of their lives.

As a nation, we have lost control. One symptom of this is our government by bureaucracy. We've become listless about our own affairs. Our political vitality has all but disappeared. We are more than willing to let someone else manage the country for us. We will gladly submit to this even if we dimly perceive our nature being distorted by gentle oppression and our vital interests being threatened by a mechanism which cannot identify these interests, let alone fight for them. Bureaucracies fight only for themselves.

If this problem were limited to the world of politics, many of us would try to ignore it. Not surprisingly, it isn't. Politics is only one activity in which our disabilities express themselves. We can see them more easily and trace their ravages more clearly in our economic system.

If we are willing to accept the truth about ourselves now, it is not only because of the obvious failure of attempted alliances of languages and cultures. Our economic failure is even more striking.

5.
Poor Little Rich Nation

Our real earnings are declining. Almost a million people in this nation of 22 million are out of work, many of them chronically unemployed. Inflation erodes our standard of living. Business activity is crippled by high interest rates. Our economy is weakening.

We see this as a specific and isolated problem in the same, fragmented way that we perceive our political difficulties. We explain it as part of a global problem. We blame others for it, particularly the United States. And our response to this economic decline is the same as our response to the political weakening of our country. We feel the same sense of hopelessness. There is no more effective national control in the management of our economy than there is in the running of our political affairs.

This double failure isn't coincidental. It stems from the same source and many of its symptoms, in the worlds of politics and business, are identical. In each case, there has been a timid response to competition. The freedom of the marketplace has driven us into the same protective crouch as has the challenge of political freedom. In business and politics, we have come to prefer the careful management of bureaucrats to the adventurous creativity of entrepreneurs.

The results have been even more damaging economically than politically, although the prosperity of recent decades has masked them, just as the stability of our political system has hidden many of its defects. Prosperity and stability are now threatened at the same time, compounding our problems.

The auto industry is the most striking example of large-scale developments creating special havoc among us and of our limited ability to respond to them. At the moment, thousands of auto workers in Canada are out of work, many of them permanently. The closing down of auto assembly plants and parts factories throughout central Ontario is creating an economic weakness that will affect the entire country for years. These workers were well-paid and protected by a wide range of union benefits. Their purchasing power was considerable; their tax contributions to the economy significant.

Car and truck plants in Ontario have suffered from a decline in the market for North American cars. Canadian plants were affected by a weak car market in the United States, even when Canadian sales remained high, because much of their production was sold in the United States within an automobile "common market." This close commercial arrangement has persuaded many Canadians that Ontario's problem is simply an aspect of a North American problem, too big for us to attack. We simply have to wait until the Americans solve it. With that kind of faulty perception, it isn't surprising that we arrive at conclusions leading nowhere.

Many of the problems of Canada's auto industry, in fact, are distinctive. They have been foreseen for years. After the Auto Pact was signed in 1965, the industry became more specialized. Before that, the Canadian auto industry was a miniature version of the American one with its own management, financial planning, and engineering services, as well as some research and development functions. In the interests of efficiency, the industry under Auto Pact expanded production facilities in Canada but moved most other functions home to plants in the United States.

Employment in Canada increased as the continental market expanded, but there were critics of the agreement. Before the North American car market slumped at the end of the past decade, the Science Council of Canada was among groups claiming that the location of research, design, and engineering facilities in the United States was costing Canada 1,400 engineering jobs along with 2,800 support staff. There was also a growing deficit in auto parts, up to an annual rate of $4 billion in 1979, which represented about 19,000 lost jobs, according to the parts manufacturers.

In effect, all the "brains" of the industry had been located in the United States, where the ownership resided. We wound up doing little in this country but bolting together cars and trucks according to the instructions provided by others. When the industry was prosperous, we bolted together more cars and trucks and made more money, but nothing else happened. We were like the workers who stay in the same place in the assembly line, earning good money but paying for it in loss

51

of ambition, motivation, imagination, and, eventually, the desire to improve themselves.

In the 1970's, as the Auto Pact deficit grew, we were worried enough to want to take a second look at the agreement. This review was undertaken by Simon Reisman, an Ottawa consultant who had been one of the bureaucrats responsible for Auto Pact in the first place. As everyone expected, he admitted that there were some problems but counselled against trying to re-negotiate the agreement at that time.

When the industry went into steep decline, when the large companies started to cut their losses by consolidating their operations, the only bargaining lever that remained to us was the money we had in our pockets – our diminishing ability to buy American cars. Our politicians went to Washington to try to use this leverage to protect us. We had lost the entrepreneurial capacity to compete and to protect ourselves.

The politicians returned from Washington with the news that this, too, was not the time to re-negotiate the Auto Pact. Good times or bad, it never seemed to be the right time to assert ourselves.

Preoccupied with the traumatic lay-offs of thousands of Ontario workers, we are now missing out on the few benefits of this depressed phase of the industry. Research and development, non-existent in the Canadian branch plants, is the only part of the industry that is booming, along with the engineering and design services needed to retool plants to produce smaller and more efficient cars. We have missed this boom once and for all, making it more impossible than ever for us to have at least the option of our own car industry to use in the future as a bargaining lever with the United States. Now our plants remain idle, waiting for the new designs and machinery to arrive from the United States so that we can go back to work on the assembly line.

The empty car plants and their limited future are typical of our industrial decline and our endangered prospects. Many of our best economic critics in the past have blamed this situation on foreign ownership of our economy. This has been a constant theme of economic and political debate, but the arguments seem to go around in circles, frantically during difficult economic times such as these, more academically and gracefully when the borrowed dollars flow more freely. We make almost no progress in resolving the problem and, curiously, those who describe it most accurately are relegated in the long run to irrelevance.

Among these critics, Walter Gordon provides the best example of the fate that seems to befall all of them because he has been the most perceptive and influential. He was the first modern economic nationalist to be entrusted with the finance portfolio in Ottawa, in the government of Lester B. Pearson in the early 1960's. His first budget expressed his philosophy and, partly because of tactical errors, became a political disaster. From that high point, Gordon's influence diminished, despite his books criticizing our economic performance and his directorship on the *Toronto Star*, which shared many of his views. Today he is admired by a small circle of disciples in Toronto, but most Canadians, if they still recognize the name, would feel that his accomplishments have been small compared with his objectives. He has been swimming against the current all his life and it has overwhelmed him, along with the rest of us.

It could almost be said that Gordon and his followers have suffered the special kind of dishonour that we assign to prophets who have failed to move us with their pronouncements. These prophets have been without influence and almost without honour in their own country. They have warned us about our failures; in rejecting them, we have turned them into failures. I have often wondered how this could have happened, if they were right. Surely they would have earned at least our anger as a mark of accomplishment if they had discovered the real reason for our failures. Their impotence and irrelevance signifies their own shortcoming – by blaming our failures on foreign domination of our economy, they have mistaken a symptom of our national malaise for its cause.

The domination of our economy by outsiders is simply another sign of our national weakness, like the fungus that attacks feeble plants in a garden while the healthy ones are able to resist. Those who have worried about the fungus, who have not been bemused by the vitality of the fungus itself, have spent most of their time pruning and spraying and propping up. It's been a losing battle and they have looked, even to their admirers, a little ridiculous. They have accomplished nothing. Canada today has the highest level of foreign control of any industrialized country in the world, with 59 per cent of our manufacturing industry controlled by foreigners. Of the 200 corporations in Canada with the largest sales volumes, 60 per cent are foreign-controlled. Between 1956 and 1976, the proportion of our corporate financing done abroad increased from 28 to 45 per cent.

Outsiders own not only the largest but the best parts. Foreign ownership of many of our old and troubled industries, such as clothing and furniture, is less than 20 per cent. In newer and expanding industries,

53

such as chemicals, machinery, and transportation equipment, it is more than 70 per cent. Our petroleum and coal industries have come within a fraction of 100 per cent foreign ownership. Nothing that we have attempted has altered this pattern. The establishment of the Foreign Investment Review Agency in 1974 has done little but enable bureaucrats to place their official stamp of approval on the process. It has not significantly changed the picture of foreign ownership in our country.

If the picture has become more complex in the past few years, it is not because of any national decisions that we have made. It has been a question, as usual, of things happening to us. While foreign ownership has remained high in the 1970's, foreign investment has declined rapidly and steadily. Canada has become less attractive to foreign investors while foreign corporations already established here have been able to earn or find enough money in this country to continue expanding.

Foreign ownership has reached a takeoff point where it can continue to grow with little help from outside. Our economy has "matured" to the point where it can finance, out of its own resources, the final takeover by outsiders. We can now be bought by foreigners with our own money. Our main concern, at this stage, seems to be ensuring that foreigners continue to do this. We are becoming alarmed now that newer, undeveloped countries may attract the interest and capital of foreign corporations who find us growing old and cranky. Our own corporations are showing less confidence in our future and are investing increasing amounts not only in undeveloped countries but in the United States. In fact, Canadians now invest more abroad than foreigners invest in Canada. Americans are debating resolutions in Congress to protect the United States against the inroads of Canadian businessmen, citing Canadian restrictions on foreign investment as a precedent.

There has been a massive deterioration of Canada's trade balance in the past five years. Our performance as an exporter of manufactured goods remains weak while imports take over a larger and larger share of our domestic market. We maintain a reasonably prosperous economy and stable currency only by continuing to increase our exports of raw materials. Servicing the dividends and interest of our foreign investment now drains $2.5 billion from our economy every year, forcing us to sell more and more of our diminishing natural resources to others. Processing these resources in our own country and exporting manufactured goods has been our stated objective for decades, but we have progressed in exactly the opposite direction. Some authorities have said this now costs us about 400,000 lost manufacturing jobs, more than enough, with the spin-off these jobs would provide, to eliminate unemployment in our country.

Disturbing as this cross-section of our economic problem is, the trend is terrifying. We are losing ground rapidly as a developed, industrial society. Our manufacturing industries now provide a smaller proportion of Canadian employment than they did thirty years ago. Critics such as John Shepherd of the Science Council have been talking about the "deindustrialization" of Canada.

For years we have puzzled over the industrial development of European countries with populations of modest size, wondering why we haven't been able to innovate, specialize, and compete internationally as they do. Now we face the prospect of being unable to compete with the manufacturing industries of Third World countries and we show the same dumb astonishment.

The pattern of the car industry – brawn in Canada and brains somewhere else – is repeated in many sectors. More than 90 per cent of the patents in force in Canada are held in other countries. Our output per man-hour is 20 per cent lower than in comparable American industries. Our national investment in research and development in relation to our gross national product is less than half that of countries such as West Germany, Japan, the United States, and the Netherlands. It has been decreasing in the past decade, from 1.26 per cent of our GNP in 1971 to 1.03 per cent in 1976. Consequently we have become less innovative and competitive than other countries. The harder it is for us to compete, the less money we have for product improvement, and the whole nation enters the kind of downward spiral familiar to many failed businessmen.

In most areas of industrial activity, we have relied on American technology. Despite the depressing effect this had on our own development, at least we had the satisfaction of relying on the best. Now the Americans are worried about competition from abroad, particularly from the Japanese, and we are both intrigued and frightened when we encounter Americans who now sound like us. They are worried about the 400,000 Japanese workers who are assigned to research and development, 50 per cent more than in the United States in relation to population. The Japanese, a nation of great savers, now invest twice as much in their economy in proportion to their GNP as do the Americans, and they invest in technological development that will pay off in the long term rather than in fast-food chains, entertainment, and other favourites of American investors that produce quick profits but little base for future development.

Some Americans who are concerned about this development have attributed it to a "faltering of will" in American society. J. Baranson, a Washington policy researcher, used that term in 1979 in speaking to a Montreal seminar sponsored by the Institute for Research on Public Policy. He said that Americans are "losing their grip" and "do not want to hear this."

"They do not evaluate what they are from within," he stated. "There are too many people around who are saying things to project some small or large institutionalized self-interest. They are also saying things that they want to hear themselves saying and that they want others to think of them as saying."

Dr. Baranson's criticism sounds to Canadian ears like an analysis of our own traditional attitudes. He claimed that the United States is being taken over by "accountants with their profit-centred minds," that "the minority voice in management, seeking to get management to take the longer term, the harder, more difficult risks, has been badly eroded."

This recent, aberrant condition in the United States is the picture we Canadians have come to accept as chronic in our own economy. By American standards, we have always had a high proportion of account- ants among our chief business executives, men who are "generally thought to be adverse to uncertainty," according to a recent federal study of Canadian business. Other authorities have referred to the dom- inant business class in Canada – bankers, financiers, and traders – as "the Lombards of Canada" after the banking dynasties of northern Italy in the thirteenth century. At the 1979 seminar addressed by Dr. Baranson, Z.P. Zeman of the Institute for Research on Public Policy said that the "deep conviction of the Lombards of Canada is that it is not so important to have our own technological capability: it is always possible to trade our abundant resources for the technological products needed to live well." He said this interpretation was supported by the "dominant position of the Department of Finance in our system of government and in the way economists have gained the upper hand over technologists" in running our affairs.

This type of leadership would explain Ottawa's lack of concern over technological issues, our failure to invest in research and development, and our inability to perceive (let alone protect) our long-term economic interests. That we have this type of leadership is evident from the way political and business decisions are co-ordinated in Canada, and the structures we have to conceal and shelter this accommodation are further evidence.

The most perfect, obvious, but least understood of these is the Canadian Senate. A colonial descendant of Britain's House of Lords, appointed by the federal government, the Senate originally was intended to protect regional interests. Its ineffectiveness has led to many proposals for its reform or abolition. Canadians generally regard the Senate as something of an antique joke, a haven for political hacks. The Senate, however, is neither as inactive nor as powerless as Canadians assume. It is the most effective business lobby in the country. Many of its members hold directorships in the business world, without the restrictions on conflicting interests that govern cabinet ministers. In the Senate, the activities of corporate lobbyists move from the vestibules of Parliament into the legislative chambers where the lobbyists are paid from the public purse and protected from any public reviews of their services at elections.

These services can be invaluable to the business community. In 1971, for example, when Ron Basford, Minister of Consumer and Corporate Affairs, introduced the Competitions Act in the House of Commons, businessmen used the Senate as a platform for much of their opposition to this attempt to make Canadian business more competitive. They were in congenial surroundings when they appeared before the Senate committee examining the bill because the chairman of the committee, Senator Salter Hayden, was one of its foremost critics. When he was chairman of the committee, he was also a member of a large Toronto law firm which represented clients appearing before his committee to oppose the bill.

Despite their age, outside interests, and security of tenure, Senators can move with remarkable speed and determination when Parliament considers legislation affecting banks or other major corporations. And it is all done smoothly and quietly within the plush confines of the Senate's Red Chamber on Parliament Hill, in keeping with the "elegant understatement" that a group of academics recently described as the chief characteristic of relations between political and commercial power in Canada, compared with the "dramatic overstatement" of the Americans. These academics at the University of Western Ontario, in a 1976 book on government regulation, portrayed the management of our affairs in Ottawa as "the politics of keeping things pleasant, dull and controlled." They stated that "influence comes from very private meetings with very important people. Public displays of power and verbal abuse are vulgar and should be shelved."

Another student of Ottawa politics, W.T. Stanbury of the Institute for Research on Public Policy, has concluded that "there does not exist in Canada any fundamental belief in the virtues of competition as a method of allocating scarce resources . . . our more structured, authoritarian society takes business power for granted."

These structures and attitudes have created an inferior executive class in Canadian business. They earn only about 75 per cent as much as American executives and they may not be worth even that. Their inclination is to look for the largest margin of safety and the smallest element of risk; their ambition is to avoid business competition as effectively as Canadians escape serious political conflict; their ideal is the world of Canadian banking dominated by a small number of large banks which restrain domestic competition as vigorously as they oppose attempts to let foreign banks into Canada.

The timid subservience of Canadian businessmen has been blamed, as one might expect, on the Americans. Managing branch plants, it has been said, has trained our executives to take orders, not to give them. If so, our aptitude for this role suggests that we have taken to it naturally, that we are more at home in the bureaucracies of business as well as politics than at the higher levels where decisions are made.

But this cautious mentality protects us only in isolated groups and within narrow limits. It loses sight of our larger interests as a national community and leaves us vulnerable in the most vital areas. Even Canadian bankers who run corporations that are large by international standards have an inclination to serve even larger business groups outside the country rather than to run the risks of taking a leading role in backing smaller Canadian enterprises against foreign competition. Serving as an instrument of foreign enterprise has made Canadian banks larger and richer at the expense of our own talent and enterprise.

Not believing in our own ability, we compete ineffectively in overseas markets. Our businessmen have always been criticized as poor salesmen. One trade minister after another in Ottawa has lectured the business community for its passive approach to foreign markets. Millions are spent on overseas trade missions and exhibits. Brilliant export possibilities are always just ahead of us or collapsing behind us: we are going to dominate trade in the West Indies; we are going to beat the Americans into Cuba or China; we are going to industrialize Latin

America. We always come back home like Willy Loman, enacting our own national version of *Death of a Salesman* over and over again.

Even when we have a better mousetrap, we only catch our own fingers in it. Or break it into pieces, as we did with the Arrow jet fighter twenty years ago. The immortal Arrow – it barely flew but it remains the most memorable aircraft this country has ever produced, a jet fighter so far ahead of its time that we had to kill it before it scared us to death.

We continue to produce books, magazine articles, and television documentaries about it. The argument about the Arrow goes on forever because, even after all these years, we find it hard to distinguish between immediate profit and our long-term national interest. By all our usual tests, the decision to scrap the Arrow was the right one because its development was proving too expensive for us, we were uncertain of our ability to sell it to others, and it seemed safer to buy American planes and to manufacture parts of them here under supervision. Still, we can't help wondering, whenever we spend billions of dollars for more American planes, whether we then made the right decision. As in the car industry, it meant that our brains, creativity, and skills counted for almost nothing in providing the best defence for our country at the most reasonable cost. All we had left to bargain with was our purchasing power. We had to rely on bureaucrats and politicians to bargain for us.

The same people have been trying with little success to interest other countries in our nuclear technology. By all accounts, the CANDU nuclear reactor is one of the best in the world, and it should be. We were building reactors at Chalk River, Ontario, during the Second World War before the atomic bomb made most other countries aware of the potential of nuclear development. Using our own technology, we have built reactors that are among the largest and safest in the world. But even with the payment of bribes and commissions in strange quarters in various countries, all documented by inquiries in Ottawa, we have been able to sell the CANDU only to a small number of countries, some of them suspected of wanting to turn our nuclear ploughshare back into an atomic sword.

The disappointment of CANDU tells us as much about ourselves as the immolation of the Arrow. It was the product of state enterprise, a form of activity congenial to us ever since the building of our national railways, the foundation of our major public utilities, and the creation of our first radio and television networks. We showed great inventive-

59

ness and technical skill in perfecting it. But when the time came to utilize it, we seemed to lose our nerve. We showed none of the entrepreneurial skills that had been so evident in some of our businessmen immediately before and after Confederation. At this critical point in a specific development, the state revealed itself to be a flawed instrument, incapable of achieving our objectives: CANDU, like the Arrow, is a political failure. We keep looking for technical explanations for our lack of success in many areas of enterprise. They have nothing to do with a failure of skill. All the failures reflect a failure of national will.

If we cannot achieve a consensus on our nature as a country, we cannot hope to agree on the nature and purpose of any national task, even the most trivial. We will always fall short of our expectations and our potential. We continually identify the wrong problems because we can't face up to the real one; then we wonder why our solutions either achieve nothing or intensify our problems.

When we compare ourselves and the Japanese, for instance, we analyse productivity per man-hour, we study different social institutions, we examine the close relations between Japanese government and business. We never discuss the principal and determining difference between ourselves and the Japanese. It isn't difficult to identify. It can be seen in the different approaches to limiting foreign investment. We do it cautiously and ineffectively, citing various technical standards we have invented to judge whether or not a foreign enterprise contributes to our well-being. The Japanese keep out foreign investors because they know instinctively what Japan is and they don't understand how it could ever be anything else. To open Japan to large amounts of foreign investment, to have segments of the Japanese economy dominated by foreign money, would be so un-Japanese as to be inconceivable.

An academic term for this basic element of the Japanese system is "consensual cultural value." Everyone in Japan agrees, without having to think about it, that their system suits them and that outsiders, not being able to feel the same about it, would threaten it. In the best restaurants in Japan, they often politely refuse to accept Western customers unaccompanied by Japanese because the clash of alien languages, customs, and eating habits would create chaos in the restaurants, mutual embarrassment, and acrimony.

In Canada, we never turn away a customer. We have no cultural value that we hold in common, no agreement on whatever it is we are trying to protect from outsiders. Our regulations against foreign investment are ineffective because they have no political foundation. Our attempts to blame our problems on foreign ownership miss the point. We are the ones who are responsible. The problem is not the weakness of our defences but doubts about what we are defending.

All our practical difficulties stem from this uncertainty about who we are. Political pressure to protect us from foreign investment or trade competition is always fragmented. Worry about American investment, for instance, has been largely an Ontario concern, echoed faintly by a few activists in the Maritimes and western provinces. In Quebec, the "foreigner" most often regarded with suspicion is the English-speaking Canadian businessman. Defending their own cultural values from the constant onslaught of the majority, after the breakdown of the first Confederation, has left Quebecers little time to worry about dangers from the United States.

Without agreement about our own nature and destiny, we have been defenceless. The invasion of foreign investment is simply the inevitable result of this loss of control. Unable to chart our own course, we have tied ourselves to the nearest thing that moved, to the American leviathan, feeding on its momentum, dragged along in its wake. This has not been enough to hold us together. Beneath all the prosperity, the process of internal disintegration has advanced with cancerous rapidity.

The elements that were joined together in the Confederation of 1867, and in the newer provinces, are now separating. We are starting to move backwards in history. The political disintegration of Canada is well-advanced.

6.
Disintegration of Leadership

Disintegration of our political system is so advanced that we are losing our ability to make important national decisions. Some of the provinces of our Confederation have become so powerful, politically as well as economically, that they now challenge the authority of the central government. In no other federal system do states or provinces possess this potent combination of wealth, political jurisdiction, and bureaucratic capacity. It has been said that Canadian provinces now are more powerful than most of the member states of the United Nations.

The central government in Ottawa is at this time engaged in a protracted and inconclusive struggle with the provincial government of Alberta over oil. In no other major oil-producing country is the oil considered to be anything but a national resource. In our country, the constitution gives natural resources to the provinces. If a province wishes, it can withhold these resources or the wealth that they generate from Canadians living in other provinces.

That this provincial right would endure under any conditions is, of course, unthinkable. The constitution also gives the federal government the right to take measures to ensure national survival. This right now seems so remote to Canadians compared with the demands of the provinces that there is some question about Ottawa's ability to exercise it. When the spirit of national consensus has become that weak, the nation has reached a dangerous stage of dissolution.

Already there are many barriers to the free flow of trade and people within Canada. Workers from Ontario do not have equal access to jobs in Newfoundland's new offshore oil industry. Contractors in Ontario encounter barriers when bidding for jobs in Quebec. Provinces structure their own purchasing policies to create what amounts to a system of special tariffs within Canada. The right of Canadians to purchase land in their own country has been questioned. Students from one province may not have equal access to universities in another province. As we accept the multiplication of these barriers, we become what many people already have described as a loosely linked series of semi-independent states, a "balkanized" nation. Government services are duplicated in almost every sector. Bureaucracies expand and compete with one another. Our internal rivalries consume more and more of our political energy. We lose sight of our real problems.

Our political structure now resembles a nuclear pile where the energy has no constructive outlet. The process of fission becomes hotter until it begins to consume the structure itself. As a nation, we are now approaching meltdown; red lights flashing, alarm bells ringing, panic in the control room, and consternation among the populace. And no evacuation is possible. If we lose control, we will simply have to live with the aftermath.

Already the excesses of government running almost out of control contaminate our existence. On a national level, the struggle of federal and provincial governments over major sources of tax revenue handicap our development. Energy projects vital to our future are endangered not because there is a lack of capital, skill, or resources but because two levels of government have lost sight of the common good in the battle for their particular interests. This struggle for supremacy between our governments complicates and distorts every aspect of Canadian life. Federal and provincial income taxes are collected, their division between the two levels of government occupying the ingenuity and energy of generations of politicians and legions of bureaucrats. In Quebec, taxpayers fill out two income tax forms as a mark of their dual allegiance and pay higher taxes in total for the privilege. Provincial rates of sales tax differ absurdly, the economies of poorer provinces carrying the extra burden of high sales taxes while consumers of the wealthiest province, Alberta, pay none. Businessmen are harassed by regulations and paperwork originating at three levels of government – federal, provincial, and municipal – often working at cross purposes. Our athletes play on battlefields of conflicting government subsidies: the right to sell a simple lottery ticket, with the proceeds going to sports and recreation, is so complex in this country that it can become a major theme of federal parliamentary debate for years.

The notion that government is designed to serve the people is quickly forgotten as our over-governed society staggers under the burden of competing interests. The more government we have, the less direction we receive.

In the past two decades, provincial governments have been in the ascendant. In 1960, provincial spending accounted for only 24 per cent of all government spending. That was the year when the election of Jean Lesage in Quebec symbolized the beginning of the "Quiet Revolution" in that province. Quiet it may have been but cheap it was not, and Quebec's pattern of growing provincial ambition and competence was soon duplicated in every province. By 1968, when Pierre Trudeau became Prime Minister, the provinces' share of public spending had risen to 33.2 per cent while Ottawa spent 40.5 per cent and local governments 26.3 per cent. By 1979, provincial spending was roughly equal to the federal share: 39.9 per cent compared with Ottawa's 39 per cent.

The struggle over money was reflected in a headlong race to administer every aspect of human activity that conceivably could be subject to government regulation, before a rival level of government discovered it. More new federal laws regulating different kinds of economic activity were passed from 1970 to 1978 than in the previous thirty years, but the 140 federal regulatory laws on the books in 1978 were far outnumbered by 1,608 provincial laws regulating economic activity.

In the decades immediately after Confederation it was the other way around. The central government was supreme in theory and fact. The first government budgets after Confederation show that Ottawa supplied more than half of the provinces' revenue from its own sources. Its own spending was many times greater than the budgets of all provinces combined. Provincial governments had modest revenues and, for the most part, local preoccupations. The regulatory laws of Ontario covered only 703 pages in 1887. By 1970, they filled a 3,085-page volume. Quebec's regulatory laws increased from 638 pages in 1888 to 2,519 pages in 1977. Much of this growth has been recent. Between 1970 and 1978, the number of regulations in Ontario grew at an average annual rate of 9.5 per cent. In Quebec from 1972 to 1978 the rate of "inflation" in the process of adopting new government regulations was 16 per cent a year.

In the past two decades, all of us have become aware of the provinces as a distinctive and competitive element in the control of our national affairs. Provincial premiers now meet regularly to discuss national concerns, almost as if they constituted a parallel national cabinet. These private sessions have become an accepted part of our government structure. Most of us have forgotten that they were an innovation of the 1960's, inspired by the hectic expansion of provincial ambition and activities in Quebec and the response of other provinces. In the early years of these communal gatherings, the premiers were careful to present them publicly as high-level seminars for academic discussion of larger issues. Since then, these "think-tanks" have developed into a strategic weapon deployed against the federal cabinet.

Provincial premiers also meet regularly and in some cases exclusively with the Prime Minister. There are now premiers who deign only rarely to discuss policy with any member of the federal cabinet below the Prime Minister. At increasingly frequent intervals, the premiers come as a group to Ottawa to confront the Prime Minister over contentious national issues. When these sessions are public, they are held in the federal Conference Centre and carried live on national television. The usual seating arrangement is around a circular conference table with the Prime Minister at some point on the circumference that may or may not be recognized as the head of the table. These federal-provincial conferences are now a new type of national parliament. Our constitution makes no mention of them. They make decisions of central importance to the country without the scrutiny and restraints of ordinary parliamentary procedure.

As anyone who has watched these conferences on television realizes, the public sessions are exercises in rhetoric. All the decisions are taken in private, usually over long lunches or dinners at the Conference Centre or at the Prime Minister's official residence. These private sessions of a self-appointed national presidium express our inability at this stage to decide our most sensitive national topics in an open and democratic forum. The running of our country apparently can no longer be entrusted to those directly elected for that task and who are responsible day by day to other elected representatives in Parliament. It has become the private business of a "board of directors," discussed over their cigarettes, cigars, and liqueur after a good meal.

Outside, under the glare of television lights, the press represent the public on the doorstep of these momentous gatherings. More often than not, the meetings end without producing agreements that can be stated in joint communiqués. The Prime Minister and the premiers go before the television cameras to give their conflicting interpretations of failure or success. Not only is the secret process confusing and destructive of public trust in government, but it is almost always futile.

The separate and contradictory statements of the premiers and the Prime Minister strengthen the public impression that here is a coalition of equal heads of state. As the limousines pull away from these inconclusive sessions bearing the premiers and their courts of advisers, the atmosphere and setting are reminiscent of times of crisis at the Security Council of the United Nations. We have come a long way in little more than a century from the vision of "one vast Confederation" that inspired McGee and his compatriots with patriotism.

Sir John A. Macdonald would have been aghast at the spectacle of provincial premiers vying with the Prime Minister for influence and authority over national affairs. His intention was to create a nation stronger than the troubled federation to the south where internal differences had produced civil war. "A strong central government is indispensable to the success of the experiment we are trying," he said in 1864. Many Canadians shared Macdonald's view. They believed that the Americans had given too much power to the states and they were determined not to repeat that mistake.

"Federation!" snorted the Montreal writer and publisher S.R. Dawson in "A Northern Kingdom," an influential pamphlet published in 1864 as the politicians were working on the terms of Confederation. "Have we not seen enough of federations with their cumbrous machinery of government, well enough in fair weather, but breaking up with the least strain – with treble taxation – with staffs of state functionaries, and of supreme functionaries, and with harassing disputes of various jurisdictions . . . ?" Dawson asked: "Must we steer our bark on that rock on which the neighbouring magnificent union has split?"

Macdonald had decided by 1866 that Americans, in creating their federation, "commenced, in fact, at the wrong end" by first considering state rights and that "this had much to do with bringing on the present unhappy war in the United States. . . . Here we have adopted a different system," he said. "We have strengthened the General Government. We have given the central legislature all the great subjects of legislation. . . . We have thus avoided that great source of weakness which has been the cause of the disruption of the United States."

Not all Canadians shared Macdonald's vision, particularly in Quebec. And many of those who supported his desire for a unified nation were not ready to work for it in a spirit of freedom and equality. They tried to find a short cut to Macdonald's objective, losing sight of it in the process. That failure to achieve Macdonald's central goal does not represent, as we have tried to pretend by all but effacing his memory, a failure in Macdonald. It is our failure.

In the past 113 years, Macdonald's dream has all but disappeared beneath an accumulation of juridical decision, precedent, and current practice that has created what he would have regarded as a nightmare. Constitutional historians trace this process in judgements made here and in Britain that confirm provincial authority over resources (the building blocks of our prosperity) and education (the framework on which our national attitudes are moulded), but these merely trace the course of contestation. The direction was inspired by our deep distrust of one another and our inability to confront our internal divisions honestly and decisively.

In periods of national emergency, the central government has regained some of its original strength. Only Ottawa, in times of economic depression, had the authority to divide the dwindling wealth of the country into fairer shares. In the Second World War, the federal government centralized all public spending. By 1944, it accounted for 86.4 per cent of national spending, leaving the provinces only 6.9 per cent and local governments 6.7 per cent. Even in wartime, this was accomplished only by accepting higher levels of political tension, particularly in Quebec where the post-war reaction was expressed in the defensive nationalism of Premier Maurice Duplessis. The nationalism of Duplessis evolved into the strident separatism of the 1960's; and that, in combination with the resource wealth and political development of many other provinces, overwhelmed federal authority and brought the process of national decision-making almost to a standstill.

Quebec was the first province to regard itself as a state within a state. The inspiration for this came from the deep sense of community shared by French-speaking Quebecers – a sentiment alien to other Canadians. Not content to call itself a nation in a symbolic fashion, as had an earlier generation by hoisting its own flag, Québécois in the 1960's set out to acquire the political apparatus of nationhood. The modern Quebec bureaucracy came into being, replacing the Roman Catholic Church as the defender of the Quebec nation.

Other provinces, already moving in the same direction, were hurried along by the example of Quebec. Provincial bureaucracies became mirror-images of the federal bureaucracy, competing with it for talent and in some cases contesting with the federal bureaucracy on equal terms. The civil servants of the new and expanding provincial states were often more ambitious, innovative, and energetic than those of the older central bureaucracy. Canadian provinces established their own quasi-diplomatic legations in other countries. In Paris during the era of President DeGaulle, there was open war between the "ambassador" of Quebec and the Canadian Ambassador, with the man from Quebec winning most of the skirmishes. This distracted attention from the burgeoning "diplomatic corps" of other provinces. By 1972 Ontario had offices in Dusseldorf, Brussels, Vienna, London, Stockholm, and Tokyo as well as in New York, Boston, Atlanta, Cleveland, Minneapolis, and Los Angeles. Provincial premiers travelled overseas as if they were capable of concluding treaties with other countries.

At home, the federal government contributed to this process by making more and more money available to the provinces without conditions. Prime Minister Pearson termed this "co-operative federalism." It meant regarding the provinces as political entities capable of administering such new social programs as pensions and medicare as well as the traditional responsibilities of education and natural resource development. In theory, the provinces were now mature enough to collaborate smoothly with Ottawa and with one another in the national interest while their smaller bureaucracies would be more efficient in administering programs.

This exercise required constant, delicate co-ordination, difficult enough at the bureaucratic level but virtually impossible amid the conflicting ambitions and changing fortunes of the political world. Trying to co-ordinate the activities of the two levels of bureaucracy became the highest bureaucratic calling, eternally frustrating, increasingly remote from political reality, voracious in terms of man-hours – in essence, an occupation approaching a certain bureaucratic ideal.

By the late 1970's, hardly an area of public policy did not involve both levels of government. Ontario's Premier William Davis was saying by 1977 that it was time to "disentangle" federal and provincial responsibilities by "bringing an end to the pervasive fragmentations, duplications and overlap that now exist in the policies and programs of the two levels of government." Quebec Finance Minister Jacques Parizeau estimated at one point that there were 150 federal-provincial committees in existence. In Ottawa, there was a standing committee of the cabinet on federal-provincial relations headed by a Secretary of State for federal-provincial relations and assisted by a special adviser to the cabinet. This was matched on the civil service side by a federal-provincial relations office in the Privy Council Office. External Affairs had a special office for federal-provincial liaison, and there was a federal-provincial division in the Department of Finance.

Ostensibly created to co-ordinate activities between Ottawa and the provinces, these federal divisions acted as intelligence corps and shock troops for their bureaucracies, warning of new incursions by provincial bureaucracies, and devising schemes to invade the few unoccupied territories in the no-man's-land between Ottawa and the provinces. All but the poorest provinces had corresponding if smaller departments. Quebec's bureaucracy, limited throughout its history to a few "great clerks" of state and a mass of political appointees, now became a new force on the Canadian scene. "There were many more of them," according to Jean-Charles Falardeau, an astute Quebec sociologist, "and, more important, their competence was such that they immediately became the most important actors on the government scene."

In the past decade, Alberta has recruited a parallel "state-bureaucratic elite," to use the description of a political scientist at the University of Alberta, L.R. Pratt. He portrayed this elite as "fiercely loyal to the province as a semi-sovereign economic and political unit and deeply engaged in the process of province-building."

It would be serious enough if we had merely turned away from the risks of a truly democratic society and turned over our public affairs to a strong central bureaucracy. Abandoning our country to a free-for-all of multiple bureaucracies in conflict is inviting disaster. Without effective political control, the bureaucrats make nonsense of our existing constitution. The weaker the constitution becomes, the more bitter and self-defeating become the bureaucratic wars.

At the same time, the federal government is crippled by the degree of economic control it already has transferred to the provinces, by the mismanagement of its own bureaucrats, and by its own attempts to retain influence with Canadians through massive spending programs. Accumulated federal deficits represent not only a drain on the country but a hobble on the freedom of the government to respond to changing conditions with new policies.

"The emperor has no clothes," as Quebec Finance Minister Jacques Parizeau said in a recent speech. "He has divested himself of all the protections which he had in financial terms. The striptease which he engaged in for the past several years has left him naked.

"Alberta has literally made off with the pot," said Parizeau. "The budgetary surplus of Alberta, at the end of this year, will be almost twice as great as the combined deficits of all the provinces, from Newfoundland to Manitoba. Alberta, at the end of this year, could eliminate all its excise taxes and personal income taxes and that would reduce its budgetary surplus by only about one-third.

"So we are in a situation where the federal government no longer has the means, no longer is able to carry out its responsibilities for redistribution of wealth, no longer is able to fulfil its responsibility to reduce regional economic differences, and at the same time we have a province which begins to have the means to play a national role."

This weakening of the federal government comes at a time when growing economic inequality between regions is making the country harder to govern. Our response to this has been to recruit larger and larger armies of bureaucrats to fight our battles for us. Instead of dealing with the original divisions and deep hatreds of our national community, the bureaucrats lose themselves in a complex labyrinth of paper – computer print-outs, position papers, agendas for action, speeches prepared for politicians. . . . The list is endless, and for the bureaucrats all this represents profit, even fun.

"Federal-provincial negotiations are coming to resemble the new brand of hockey," according to one of these bureaucrats, Max Yalden, Commissioner of Official Languages. "The pre-game posturing is more engrossing than the contest itself." Reporting in 1980 on federal-provincial negotiations in his own field of education and language training, Yalden concluded that "at year's end the negotiators were still skating around in circles with nothing to show on the scoreboard."

This form of bureaucratic employment and entertainment is no substitute for government. It makes it impossible to govern the country, even should our politicians wish to shoulder their responsibilities. But again, it is not the cause of our national failure. It is just another symptom.

Criticizing bureaucrats is now almost as popular among us as attacking Americans: the bureaucrats as the enemy within to correspond to our traditional enemy outside the walls. It's a poor substitute for examining aspects of our national failure that relate directly to us.

In every area of national activity, from industrial development to education, from health care to film production, we have performed far below our potential. Our self-destructive tendencies seem to weaken every effort that we make. It almost seems that setting our sights on an objective is enough to start us moving in the opposite direction.

7.
Inside Canada:
The Cost of Failure

Afraid to discover exactly what we are, unable to control our own affairs, we are deteriorating not only as a political structure but as a place to live. We like to think of ourselves as a prosperous, capable, and tolerant society. If we ever did correspond to this myth to some degree, the ideal is slipping into the past and fading out of our future. Even those Canadians who have little interest in the history of our political failures cannot ignore this. Our standard of living is declining, measured in terms of real wages and in relation to other developed countries. Our unemployment rate hovers stubbornly around 10 per cent of our labour force. Our annual inflation rate is about 10 per cent.

Needless to say, we aren't the only country to shudder under the impact of global recession. Many countries have suffered far more severely; a few European nations perhaps have protected themselves more effectively. Our special problem lies in our response to these difficult conditions.

The recession hit us at a time when we were losing our ability to react to challenges as a national community. This frustrated our efforts to cope with it and magnified its destructive effects, not only on our economy but on our individual natures and on the character of our society. Under stress, relatively gentle as it was, we quickly became a smaller, more selfish people.

Societies can be measured, it has often been said, by their treatment of their weakest members. By that test, we are failing. For a short time in our history, from 1930 to 1951, we did progress in distributing our national wealth more equitably. The trend has been reversed since then; our rich grow richer while our poor slip farther from any hope of recovery. The poorest one-fifth of our families had 4.4 per cent of our total wage and salary income in 1951. By 1976, their share had dropped to 4.1 per cent.

The gap between rich and poor has widened despite vast government expenditures on unemployment insurance benefits, pensions, family allowances, and myriad forms of social welfare. In addition to payments made directly to individuals by the government, there are programs to train Canadians for employment, to help them find jobs, and to create jobs for them. Many federal programs are duplicated by the provinces. As in other areas of government activity, the more programs we have, the less effective they seem to be.

Senator David Croll's Committee on Poverty in 1971 judged that our income-support and job-creation programs were excessively bureaucratic, involved a great deal of duplication, and were often ambiguous and contradictory in their objectives. Ten years later, nothing has changed except the depression of the poor, which has deepened, and the political will among the rest of us to do something about it, which has all but vanished.

Senator Croll called our welfare policies contradictory. Hypocritical would have been a more honest description. At the same time as we grudgingly spent more to help the poor, we rigged our tax system to benefit the rich. Redistribution of income through federal tax changes in the 1970's provided an additional $225 for every low-income family but it gave $968 to an average middle-income family and $3,170 to a family in the highest-income bracket.

Not only have we been losing our so-called "war on poverty," but every indication suggests that the federal government is giving up the struggle. A study of federal spending in 1980-81 by Carleton University's School of Public Administration concluded that, by 1979, the ability of the federal government to improve incomes of the poor was less than it had been ten years earlier.

Poorer regions have suffered the same fate as individuals. Despite the channeling of massive amounts of money through our various bureaucracies, the gap between the haves and the have-nots among the provinces has widened. More than ten years ago, Ottawa created a Department of Regional Economic Expansion to consolidate federal-provincial programs designed to redistribute economic opportunities in favour of our underdeveloped regions. Instead of co-ordinating our approach to this basic national problem and making it more effective, DREE became a bureaucratic expression of the inequities and inefficiencies it was supposed to reduce. Without having a political direction of its own based on national consensus, it was invaded and dominated by the problem that it had set out to conquer.

Today, DREE is our perfect Ottawa Frankenstein, a bureaucratic monster that has taken over almost the whole country except for parts of Alberta and the Toronto area. Instead of developing the poorer regions, it succeeded finally in classifying almost the entire country as underdeveloped. In the process, it became transformed to some extent into a creature of political patronage. One study in 1976 by Keith Storey of Newfoundland's Memorial University showed that regions with a long history of support for the Liberal Party have received a disproportionate share of grants. This type of welfare for provinces has been as ineffective and destructive as official charity has been for individual Canadians. The Atlantic provinces now receive from 40 to 50 per cent of their provincial revenues from elsewhere in Canada, and Quebec about 20 per cent. These client provinces of the federal government also supply much of the ruling Liberal Party's traditional support.

Such a self-defeating system is self-perpetuating and, at the same time, unstable, so fragile has our federalism become. Political loyalties tend to go to the highest bidder. Alberta is now using its vast financial resources to provide direct support for the poorer provinces, lending New Brunswick $200 million and Nova Scotia $50 million from the Alberta Heritage Fund and investigating equity investments in all the Maritime provinces. This undercuts the federal government's traditional ability to buy political support in these provinces. It has been a factor in isolating Ottawa and Ontario in the struggle with Alberta over oil and gas prices.

As our political system deteriorates during a time of economic recession, those who suffer first are the ones who live on the fringes of our society. There are more than 300,000 native citizens of Canada, the majority under thirty years of age and the vast majority unemployed. Only a generation ago, most of these native peoples were living on reserves as wards of the federal government. From 1961 to 1971, the proportion of the native population living in our cities tripled. By 1985, more than half of our native peoples will be urban, concentrated in our slum ghettos, and this is one problem for the future that we can identify now with absolute certainty.

A superficial flurry of concern for native peoples in the 1960's and early 1970's has disappeared in the tougher and more competitive society of today. We are no longer moved by compassion or frightened by threats of racial problems in the future. Our urban schools reflect this as they fail to adapt to the special needs of native children and create, in the words of Winnipeg economist Michael Decter, "a generation of children of the ghetto with deep contempt for Canadian society."

As native peoples have moved into our cities, they have become victims of the political failure that afflicts us all. In days gone by, smallpox was the white man's gift to the Indians. Now the effects of bureaucratic management destroy their prospects. In the cities, native peoples use provincial services and their welfare has become the responsibility of both the federal and provincial governments. As both levels of government haggle over who pays for native services, neither wants to undermine its bargaining position by starting new services.

Our disregard for native peoples is an international scandal that the world has yet to appreciate: Indian infant mortality is almost twice as high as in the rest of our population, 26.1 deaths per 1,000 population compared with 14.3 deaths; our native population has severe diet deficiencies; alcoholism is epidemic; crime is rampant. In Saskatchewan, only 4.5 per cent of the population outside the jails is native. Inside, 25 per cent of the prisoners are Indians.

Our native peoples we will always have with us, despite our efforts to ignore them. Immigrants whom we have trouble living with because of language, religion, or colour, we can attempt to exclude and, when that has failed, oppress. We became a less tolerant society in the 1970's, perhaps venting on new immigrants the anger and frustrations that we felt toward one another.

There was a period, from 1967 to 1978, when we briefly displayed a more open attitude. Changes in immigration regulations made it easier for non-whites to settle in Canada and thousands of them did. From 1967 to 1974, one out of every four new immigrants was black or South Asian. Most of them congregated in the larger cities. In 1970, for instance, more than 60 per cent of Toronto's new arrivals were East Indian, West Indian, or African.

This was a severe test of our humanity. As economic conditions became more difficult for all Canadians in the 1970's, we responded predictably. When the federal government issued a Green Paper on Immigration in 1975 and invited Canadians to debate the issue, it reinforced the suspicion in the minds of many Canadians that there was a connection between immigration, rising unemployment, and other signs of recession. In this way, according to a 1979 paper by Leslie Hardy of the Ontario Institute for Studies in Education, "the federal government has contributed to the tendency to blame immigrants for the country's ills."

Many of us needed little encouragement. Report after report in the late 1970's documented the existence of racism in our country. There were violent incidents in subways and parking lots and on the streets. Racial minority parents have complained that violence and racial abuse have become common in our schools. Minority groups have complained about treatment by the police.

In a 1972 *Toronto Star* survey of black immigrants from the United States, we were described as being more "polite" racists than Americans. If the blacks thought this was a sign of a more tolerant society, they were mistaken. We were simply giving them the same masked, repressed hostility that we have directed toward one another for several centuries.

In the United States, there has been blatant segregation and violence but there is also hope. There is legislation to remove barriers between races and real progress toward integration within certain economic and social limits. In Canada, we remain polite but we shall not be moved. Most of us are determined to keep contacts with people of another colour on the same formal, impersonal basis as our traditional contacts with people who speak another language.

New immigrants and native groups feel the cold shoulder of indifference and the hard edge of deprivation, but all of us, even the most prosperous and self-centred, are suffering a decline in the quality of our lives. The complex array of public services that cradles this middle-class country is deteriorating, partly because of economic recession but mainly because we are losing sight of national priorities amid the complexities of bureaucratic management.

If it were possible to buy intelligence, for example, we would now be the wisest country in the world. During the 1960's, the number of teachers in Canada increased from 175,000 to 320,000. Our spending on education rose from $1.7 million in 1960 to about $7.4 billion in 1970. In the same period, university enrolment increased by 213 per cent.

Many of the new university buildings are empty today. Changes in the birthrate in the past few decades are partly responsible for this. Perhaps more significant in the long run, our young people are skeptical about the usefulness of a university education. While enrolment in our universities may decline by as much as 15 per cent during the next decade, community colleges teaching more practical courses already are turning away 10 per cent of their applicants in some provinces.

This is not distinctively Canadian but there are reasons for it which are peculiar to us. In our schools, where our children receive the first imprint of our society outside the home, we seem to have been wandering in a no-man's-land between what used to be called "progressive" education and a more traditional type of schooling. Many of us are coming to the conclusion that what is wrong with our schools is that neither teachers nor students work hard enough. But hard work requires a clear sense of direction and a clear objective. Our whole education system today seems to be lost in a world of its own. So disoriented have our educators become that, according to one of them, we have tended in the recent past "to buy ideas that the United States has attempted and dropped as failures. These rejected concepts then form the basis of the new educational panacea for Canada," stated Ronald Cheffins, Professor of Law at the University of Victoria, in 1978.

During the past decade, while our spending on education continued to increase, the educational performance of our students has declined markedly. Surely this must have something to do with the fact that our system of education is probably the most fragmented in the world. It is divided in many places by language, religion, racial origin, and financial status and everywhere by conflicting and competing government jurisdiction. We expect the impossible when we ask a shattered school system to produce a citizen who knows where he is going, what his country should be, and what he can contribute to his society. Our schools fail to give their students even the basic instinct of an educated person, the notion that learning is a worthwhile if arduous activity in itself. That is why many of them will not and perhaps cannot go to university. As far as training them to contribute to our society, the failure is complete because we have no agreement on the nature of that society which we can give to them.

"It has not been possible to impart a sense of common history," admitted Bernard Ostry, commenting on our schools in 1978 after a career in public service devoted in large part to encouraging that awareness of history among Canadians.

The data testifying to the ignorance of our students is voluminous and depressing. A national survey of students in their last year of high school in 1975 showed that 61 per cent were unable to identify the British North America Act as our constitution. Only 71 per cent were able to name Sir John A. Macdonald as our first Prime Minister. Eight per cent picked Abraham Lincoln, an absurdity matched only by the five per cent who thought that Jimmy Carter was the Prime Minister of Canada.

"I don't want to see any more polls or surveys about how little high school graduates know about our country," said one of them, John Geiger, of Edmonton, in a letter to the editor of a small magazine this year.

"The problem lies not with the students but with the educational system and the administrators. . . . It is difficult enough for young Canadians to understand the meaning of national pride and national identity when they are constantly overwhelmed with foreign television programs. But how can we even hope to have young Canadians understand the meaning of Canada when our educational system is inept? When Canadian history is an option in high school? Physical education is compulsory in grade 10, but Canadian history is an option . . . how is that for priorities?"

Other major institutions have gone astray under the blind custody of the bureaucracy, without any guidance from society. Our bodies as well as our minds are affected. In the 1960's, with great political difficulty, we instituted a system of medical and hospital care to ensure all of us against crippling medical bills. The system instead has started to cripple the proud structure and traditions of medicine in this country, turning patients against doctors and doctors into wealthy corporations. The Carleton University survey of government spending, already mentioned, diagnosed an evident "deterioration in equality of access to medical care." There is some question as to whether doctors' demands for more money or federal-provincial conflict over health care is mainly responsible. In fact, the conflict and confusion at the top promotes selfishness among doctors, another example of "every one for himself" within a disintegrating system.

Our medical schools continue to produce a medical elite, not only for ourselves but for other countries. Up to one-quarter of the graduates from some of our medical schools are foreigners, mainly American, the others often from wealthy families in underdeveloped countries. Yet we continue to restrict, in one way or another, the enrolment of our own women in medical schools. Among Western countries, only Spain has a smaller proportion of female to male physicians than have Canada and the United States.

This type of tradition and training continues to produce a medical elite whose standard of success is the income level of doctors in the

United States. By the late 1970's, in every province except British Columbia, Newfoundland, and Quebec, doctors were attacking the foundations of state medicine by extra billing – by charging more for their services than the government paid and collecting the difference from their patients.

Although most of the money for medicare came from the central government, administration was a jealously guarded provincial field. As the bureaucrats battled, the medical system became less accessible to those of us who could not afford to pay a little extra. Confused national health policies have left us with a system of high-cost medical establishments to care for the sick and a huge bureaucracy to administer the system.

Preventive medicine, including the maintenance of a health environment for all of us, has languished. In the beginning of the 1970's, Ottawa responded to growing public awareness of environmental issues by creating a new department, Environment Canada. The Carleton University study of 1980-81 federal spending revealed that this department is "clearly in a state of eclipse." Problems created by the absence of a defined political mandate were compounded, once again, by provincial suspicions of federal actions affecting resources development and the growing financial ability of the three westernmost provinces to support their own environmental programs.

Healthy countries should produce good athletes. In most parts of the world, excellence in sports is regarded as a matter of national pride. We lost our world leadership in hockey in the 1950's, and since then we simply haven't cared, except for the 1972 Canada-USSR hockey series when we were once again the best in the world. The triumph was brief and we knew, all along, that we couldn't sustain it. That inability to persevere has been the frustration of hundreds of coaches since we increased our national spending on athletics in recent decades and created our first sports bureaucracy in Ottawa. For a time our medal count in international competition improved, but then the pace of progress slackened. There were interminable squabbles between Ottawa and the provinces over control of sports and the division of lottery proceeds used to finance it. The atmosphere in amateur sports today is poisonous. Athletes complain about lack of public support. Coaches berate the athletes for lack of discipline. There seems to be no cohesive will to win. It used to be said that the British Empire was created on the playing fields of England. Amateur sports in Canada are a sorry reflection of our political disasters.

Professional sports in this country are a branch-plant activity of the American sports industry. Our National Hockey League is dominated by American business and entertainment interests. We now have two baseball teams in the American major leagues. The ultimate triumph of American sports occurred when the opening of the current Parliament was shifted from its traditional afternoon time to the morning hours because it conflicted with the Toronto Blue Jays' first game of the season.

No field of national endeavour illuminates the gap between pretensions and performance more glaringly than culture. We have never been able to define a national culture: we have never been able to decide on whether we have one culture, one and a half, two, or an infinite number. That hasn't prevented us from spending vast amounts in attempting to discover, support, defend, and market whatever it is. In his recent book, *The Cultural Connection*, Bernard Ostry estimated that the federal government alone has spent about two per cent of its total budget in the past decade on culture, amounting currently to about a billion dollars a year. If money could buy culture, Canada would now be the envy of the world's intelligentsia. Instead, we envy many smaller and much poorer nations for their ability to express their distinctive nature and their pride in their national achievements. For all our money, we have been able to buy only bureaucratic structures to promote culture and artistic creations that advertise our divisions. Our occasional flashes of brilliance are difficult for us to perceive through all the barriers.

In my own field, television, we have lost the sense of direction that inspired the founders of radio and television in this country. The Royal Commission on Radio Broadcasting in 1929 started from the proposition that "Canadian radio listeners want Canadian broadcasting." Introducing the Canadian Radio Broadcasting Act in 1932, Conservative Prime Minister R.B. Bennett said that radio broadcasting could become "a great agency for communication on matters of national concern and for the diffusion of national thought and ideals . . . an agency by which national consciousness may be fostered and sustained and national unity still further strengthened. . . . "

Our first coast-to-coast radio network was achieved on July 1, 1927, by the state-owned Canadian National Railways. Its president, Sir Henry Thornton, according to Frank Peers in his *The Politics of Canadian Broadcasting 1921-1951*, "saw radio as a great unifying force in Canada; to him the political concept transcended the commercial, and he set out consciously to create a sense of nationhood through the medium."

This grand design failed its first real tests under the Canadian Radio Broadcasting Commission, the precursor of the Canadian Broadcasting Corporation. When it attempted French programming as part of its service to the western provinces, there was so much opposition that it had to arrange separate programming for Quebec.

"The CBC continued this policy," as Bernard Ostry has written, "so that the grand plan for national unity through radio only contributed further to creating a deeper cultural gulf between the two main language groups."

Television perpetuated this division. As a result, now that television signals are showering down on us from satellites and unauthorized receivers are starting to multiply, the national broadcasting system is crumbling at the edges and we have no firm, unified response. The federal agency that regulates broadcasting has become so entangled in red tape that it is paralyzed. We proclaim that a healthy national broadcasting system is vital to our national survival but when it is threatened, no one, quite literally, seems to know what to do.

Film-making in Canada illustrates concisely how we often set out to achieve a specific objective and then, without a clear sense of direction, quickly lose our way and find ourselves somehow moving out of control and in the opposite direction. A few years ago, we had almost no feature film industry. We adjusted our tax laws to promote one and now, to all outward appearances, we have a thriving film industry. But look more closely. What we actually have is a sponsoring government agency that spent money on yachts and champagne at the recent Cannes film festival as if it were an old-time Hollywood impresario; we have foreign producers, directors, and actors working in Canada in unprecedented numbers; we have started to produce some of the most extravagant flops the motion picture world has seen for some time. And now we are asking ourselves why we are doing all of this. What did we set out to achieve? Are we achieving it? No one seems to know.

Every field of cultural activity seems to be in trouble all the time. We spend about one-third as much as most industrial countries on book publishing, in relation to our gross national product. Despite grants from government, our publishers struggle desperately against overwhelming American competition in the marketplace and succumb, one by one, to foreign takeovers. Why we permit foreign ownership and branch-plant management in book publishing but exclude it from newspapers and electronic communication is hard to explain. Book and magazine publishing was in such a sorry condition in 1975 that the then Secretary of State, Hugh Faulkner, admitted that "one of our problems in Canada is that so many Canadians do not know and have no ready way of finding out what is being written in this country and by whom."

This depressing list could go on and on, and it does, endlessly. We never seem to tire of enumerating our disasters. We have become an introverted people, frustrated and depressed by our constant failures. We sit in a room that seems to grow smaller and darker, more and more fearful of the noise and bustle on the street outside.

8.
Outside Canada:
Advertising Our Failure

If armies reveal the natures of the countries they defend, perhaps we had better disband ours. Its message about the ability of our country to survive is as clear as if it marched under the white flag.

It is said to be the most over-officered, undermanned, ill-equipped, costly, and confused military force on either side of the Iron Curtain. It is the perfect military expression of everything wrong with us as a nation.

The top-heavy structure of our armed forces has been documented in Gerald Porter's recent book, *In Retreat*. From 1969 to 1976, personnel costs increased until they reached a staggering 66 per cent of our total military budget. No other Western nation spends such a huge share of its defence budget on manpower; in most cases, it is about half of that.

Increased salaries were part of the reason. From 1969 to 1976, an untrained private's salary rose by 160 per cent while officers' salaries almost doubled. Another, more significant reason was a wholesale movement of personnel into the upper levels of the military bureaucracy. By 1976, our unified military force had 106 generals, one for every 170 privates. The privates were outnumbered by the corporals two to one. There was one officer for every four and a half men, by far the highest such ratio in the Western world.

Not unexpectedly, our military bureaucracy displays the same characteristics as the civilian, for the same reasons and with the same results. We have tried to substitute generals for leadership, just as we have handed over political leadership of the country to the mandarins of Ottawa and the various provincial capitals. And we have discovered, in military as in civilian life, that multiplying the number and salaries of managers at the top of the system means, paradoxically, a loss of control.

The military failure, like the others, is rooted in our inability to discover and accept our true nature as a country. Not understanding ourselves, we can hardly wonder at our doubts about the value of defending ourselves or at our inability to define an international role for Canada.

This question became more urgent for Canadians at the end of the sixties, when we began to suspect that our internal divisions were hampering our ability to function on the world stage. Our international image mattered to us then.

We had been proud of ourselves under the leadership of Prime Minister Pearson. His Nobel Peace Prize and our soldiers serving as peacekeepers in many parts of the world gave us an international vocation. Perhaps it was not the major role that we might have played if we had moved aggressively onto the world stage after the Second World War, with our large merchant fleet and our industrial base intact, but it was identifiable and respectable. By 1967, Canadian troops had served or were serving on three United Nations peacekeeping forces, six United Nations peace-observation missions, and, since 1954, with the International Commissions for Supervision and Control in Vietnam, Cambodia, and Laos. This peacekeeping role was shouldered proudly by Canada.

By the end of the decade, the Trudeau government had called all this into question in a review of foreign policy. It concluded that our traditional middle-power role was outmoded. Canada would no longer be the "helpful fixer" of international conflict. Instead, we would show a more "active concern with world events." Canada's new role was more closely defined in a policy that came to be known as the Third Option. Its objective was to lessen Canadian dependence on the United States cautiously by promoting trade and diplomatic relations with other countries.

The Third Option was another of our attempts to achieve a triumph of image over reality, and it didn't work. Fooling all of ourselves all of the time perhaps was a necessary expedient at home during this period, but it wasn't exportable. Other countries regarded it as a curiosity produced by our troubled domestic politics. It had no practical effect. Our trade with Europe continued to languish. The commercial promise of the "Pacific rim" remained on the distant periphery. Despite our unhappiness over Vietnam, we were drawn even more tightly into the commercial and diplomatic orbit of the United States. And when the Americans in 1980 boycotted the Moscow Olympics over the Soviet invasion of Afghanistan, Commonwealth countries differed in their response to this and British athletes defied their government and competed in Moscow, but Canada followed Washington with more alacrity and loyalty than it often had given to London in the old days of Empire.

The Third Option was no option at all, but nothing replaced it. We continued to serve as a "helpful fixer." All we gave up was deriving any satisfaction from it. A serviceman on his way to Cyprus the other day told me that Canada wants to remove its contingent from the island but that its departure has become politically difficult, not because its peacekeeping role is essential but because the Canadian military force, after sixteen years in Cyprus, has become a major element of the local economy. That's what our peacekeeping role has become: a kind of foreign aid for Cypriot merchants.

This confusion of objectives and the pacifism of the 1960's decimated our armed forces. Defence was the Trudeau government's lowest priority. While federal spending increased from $10 billion to $45 billion from 1969 to 1978, the defence budget inched from $1.8 billion to $3.8 billion, the smallest increase of any department. Manpower in our armed forces during this period dropped from 104,000 to 78,000.

In 1973, in a paper prepared for the Canadian Institute of International Affairs, Colin S. Gray stated that "the prestige of the armed forces is low . . . the legitimacy of a military career is being widely questioned by men of recruitment age . . . and the strategic, political and economic rationales of the Canadian Forces are somewhat weak." In Europe, according to Porter, Canada's NATO force had become the "smallest, weakest and most insignificant military contribution to the Alliance." Gray entitled his paper on the military profession: The Search for Identity. Our soldiers, not surprisingly, were as lost as the rest of us.

There was, in the beginning, a positive reason for reducing our military spending, but it was never translated into reality. In his first speech as Prime Minister to the United Nations in 1968, Pierre Trudeau had outlined a plan for slowing the nuclear arms race and promoting the development of a new economic order. Nations would be asked to cut back defence spending and the money would be used for development of the Third World. We practised only part of what the Prime Minister had preached, the part that involved doing less rather than more. While our military spending decreased as a proportion of government spending, our foreign aid continued to fall short of targets set by ourselves and by the United Nations. According to a 1979 study of foreign aid by Douglas Roche, a Conservative Member of Parliament from Edmonton, Canada spends less than 0.45 per cent of its gross national product on foreign aid and the proportion is declining.

Most of us don't realize how completely the generous and fairminded image that Canada once possessed has faded. We are now regarded as being like everyone else, intent on promoting our own interest. A United Nations study of the 1963-72 period showed that we contributed $2.3 billion in official development assistance to the leastdeveloped countries during those years but also took in, through our selective immigration process, 56,000 skilled workers from these countries with an estimated capital value of $11.5 billion.

While there is some doubt about the effectiveness of our foreign aid projects in the countries that receive them, they certainly work for us. As Douglas Roche has explained, our bilateral aid in 1977-78 to the ten largest recipients of our foreign aid was $314.7 million, but $267.5 million never reached the overseas countries. It was spent here in Canada, on our insistence, to buy goods and services to send overseas. During the same period, we exported goods worth $429.7 million to these ten countries but imported only $180.2 million worth of goods from them. No matter how you look at the accounts, we came out ahead in every column.

Bureaucracy has flourished in our foreign aid as in our domestic programs. The Canadian International Development Agency, which administers most of our foreign aid, has a total staff of 1,060 but only 55 of these are in the field.

No improvement is in sight. In his first speech to the United Nations after the 1980 election, External Affairs Minister Mark MacGuigan promised not to increase foreign aid but to increase the bureaucracy in Ottawa. (In a later speech, he did set higher targets for foreign aid.) He announced the creation of a "Futures Secretariat" within CIDA which would develop a new awareness of the need for foreign aid in the Canadian public so that we could urge the government to do more. MacGuigan's speech carried our political development in this sector to its ultimate absurdity. We are now going to ask our bureaucracy not only to carry out our political wishes, but to formulate them for us.

Without knowing what we are or where we are going, we continue to blunder about the world stage, fortunately without the instincts, ability, or opportunity to do any real damage. Until we can solve our problems at home, we won't be able to improve our performance or image internationally.

We have to start at the heart of our difficulties.

9.
Montreal:
The Heart of the Problem

Montreal is no longer the largest or most important city in Canada, but it is still the heart of the Canadian problem. Forget about the rest of the country; forget about the rest of Quebec. If there were no Montreal, there would be no English in Quebec. If there were no English-speaking Quebecers, Canada as we know it today would not exist. It would be a different country, or countries, with different problems.

The old heart beats slowly now. To anyone who has known the city in better days, Montreal looks as if it is dying. It has suffered terribly in the past two decades, not to the same extent as Beirut, Belfast, or Detroit, but from the same disease. Its people have turned against one another, violently on some occasions, more often with a dull anger that silences communication and makes collaboration impossible.

In concert with the rest of the country, Montreal glimpsed a new kind of future during the centennial year, when Expo 67 showed what we could accomplish together. There was a glimmer of the same spirit during the 1976 Olympics. But in the long, barren stretches between these expensive festivals, businesses moved away from the city, the harbour and airports stagnated, and depression hung over Montreal as palpably as the heavy, acrid mist from its flaring refineries in the east end.

Last summer, its autocratic Mayor declared another international festival, Floralies 80, and he transformed the old Expo islands in the St. Lawrence River into the largest flower garden in the world. Amid the refuse from the only major city in Canada that purifies none of its sewage but pumps it all into that majestic sewer, in the shadow of the charred black cage that was the framework of the geodesic dome that Buckminster Fuller designed for the American exhibit at Expo 67, with the city dying across the water, Floralies 80 looked like a vast funeral barge covered with flowers.

The heart beats slowly, but obituaries are premature. Montreal will never be the same again, it is true, but there are signs that the city can live again, in a new form. It has endured the agony that all of us are about to suffer and it has survived. Its people have faced the truth about themselves. They have lost the illusions we still cherish. They have glimpsed the real face of Canada – it has been a horrifying experience – but they have endured. The city is quiet now, exhausted, depressed, but there are stirrings of new life.

Montreal is not only a symbol of our failure as a nation, the first and chief victim of this failure, but it may also be a symbol of resurrection. If we see it as such, perhaps it will be. But walking through the city now, it's hard to have faith in the future or to remember its glorious past. The old city along the harbour has not justified the optimism of its commercial restorers. In the 1960's, expensive boutiques and elegant restaurants started to renovate a waterfront that had been abandoned decades earlier to derelicts and flop houses. The restaurants are still there but newer ones have failed to appear, and the boutiques look faded and tacky. The business and financial centre that started to develop around Place Ville Marie is stillborn. Further east along Dorchester Boulevard, huge office buildings financed mainly by government rob the surrounding slums of sunlight and of any pretensions of quaintness. The great department stores along St. Catherine Street trail nondescript skeins of cheap novelty shops, hamburger joints, and dirty movie houses. Little is left of the nineteenth-century greystone terraces along Sherbrooke Street, and that little has stagnated. There are few new stores or art galleries worth noticing. The growth of existing galleries has been expressed in new branches in Toronto or Calgary.

The comparison with Toronto is devastating. Toronto on a summer day in 1980 seemed to swelter in a golden mist, a heavy blend of gasoline and money. The city is competent and works hard. The stores are filled with luxury goods to reward this diligence. Toronto's aims are as immediate and straightforward as its Tower. It has everything it wants in the present and there is a feeling that if the future is located somewhere else, the city will simply move there.

Montreal doesn't seem to be going anywhere. St. James Street, once the financial centre of Canada, is filled with rental signs. Old brokers' premises are occupied by discount stores. Halfway along what is now called rue St. Jacques, the Gothic facade of an old office building marks the tomb of The Montreal Star. The voice of the street was the last thing to go in 1979.

Character the city still has. At night, she can still look like a dowager empress. She can be witty and seductive even if the masquerade is harder to sustain nowadays. Montreal can still be loved. There is still pleasure in her company and conversation.

How beautiful she must have been in her prime. The men who built Canada in the nineteenth century endowed her with gracious public buildings and private mansions. She was a fit residence in those days for these creative and competitive spirits. The new commercial districts rising above the narrow streets of the harbour had broad avenues and squares that reminded visitors of European capitals. In the residences along the heights of Dorchester Boulevard, drawing rooms were filled with the finest furniture from England and the United States as well as from the studios of local craftsmen; libraries displayed the latest editions from London, New York, and Paris; wine cellars were stocked with the best European vintages and boxes of truffles from France; orange trees bloomed in conservatories, and on the slopes behind the houses apple orchards gave way to distant views of the St. Lawrence curving about the island.

Ocean liners linked Montreal's harbour to Europe. Rail connected the city to the United States, to the winter ports of the Maritimes and New England, to Ottawa and Toronto and the expanding territories of the West. Industries congregated near the hubs of these continental and international networks.

The city culminated in a wild park that covered the low mountain in the centre of the island. There were snowshoe races through the forest in the wintertime high above the lights of the city. In the summer, as the park was tamed in this century by the same landscape architect who gave Central Park to New York, there were walks on the shores of an artificial lake and picnics on the bluffs facing north toward the dark green ridges of the Laurentians.

The first Canadian libraries, museums, and theatres were built in Montreal. McGill University developed a renowned medical school. One of McGill's economics professors, Stephen Leacock, wrote humorous stories and essays that delighted the world. There were the beginnings of an intellectual tradition. In the compressed mass of students and immigrant workers in the streets between McGill University and the old Jewish ghetto on St. Urbain Street, radical political theories from Europe received a North American stamp. The seeds of Canadian socialism were sown, to germinate later on the western prairie. Eventually it was a city that could produce as complex a character as Dr. Norman Bethune, aristocratic spirit and radical intellectual, physician at the birth of the new China, the only Westerner in the pantheon of Chinese Communism.

English and French-speaking Montrealers lived in their separate worlds; respected the differences that separated them; took pride in their own traditions and achievements; regarded one another, in the main, without hostility and even with some affection.

Conflicting versions of those decades before 1960 make it difficult to understand what it was really like. Many English-speaking Montrealers remember it as a halcyon period when English and French existed together in harmony. On the French-speaking side, the orthodox interpretation of this period pits French against English in a city divided by class and language. Somewhere between these two extremes lies the true Montreal of the first half of this century.

That the English dominated the city is not surprising. They formed almost half the population at one time and controlled more than their share of business activity. At best, they were paternalistic about the French; at worst, discriminatory in a ruthless, automatic way.

There were also good relations between French and English within narrow limits, of a warmth and cordiality unknown today. Lineage and wealth often overlooked barriers of language and even religion in the uppermost level of society. There were marriages between wealthy French and English and one of them produced our current Prime Minister. Neither side felt inferior to the other. Each admired the other's better qualities, expressing in their personal lives, and under ideal material conditions, the dream of Macdonald and Cartier.

French-Canadian intellectuals chafed at the subordinate position of their community and took refuge in its spiritual superiority, but how much of this reached the ordinary French-Canadian worker or office clerk is hard to determine. French-speaking society had its own class divisions, more impenetrable than the English. The people at the bottom were farmers, tradesmen, and the workers who were emigrating from the villages into the cities. At the top were the rural descendants of the seigneurial families, the clergy, lawyers, notaries and doctors, politicians and a small number of businessmen in the larger centres.

It must have been a bit like Victorian England. Social status could be determined by the way one spoke. There was a network of private colleges to replenish the ranks of the elite. The schools were spartan and authoritarian and they gave their students a clear idea of their own obligations to society and Quebec society's special place in the affairs of man and God.

It must also have been a little like pre-Revolutionary Russia. On summer holidays, the students would return to family estates to renew their national identity in the unchanging routines of farm and village. The upper class was filled with little Tolstoys who dreamed of a society resting on the docile shoulders of healthy peasants. While they dreamed, Québécois abandoned their poor farms to move into the cities and to fight for jobs at the lowest level against immigrants arriving from overseas.

The conflicts and wounds of the past two decades are too fresh to allow either side to see the past accurately. No one has yet written a sympathetic history of this period in Quebec that does justice not only to the French-speaking aristocrats who gave tone and character to their society, but also to the energy, creativity, and colourful personalities of English-speaking Quebec. When that special aspect of Quebec's history can be written accurately and appreciatively by French-speaking historians, it will be conclusive evidence of maturity.

In our parents' generation in Quebec, most people assumed this comfortable world would endure forever. At the same time, they were doing their best to destroy it. On the French side, the rigorous training of a classical education produced both staunch defenders of the existing order and formidable opponents critical of their own society and aware of developments in other countries. While the French-speaking elite inadvertently educated the revolutionaries of tomorrow, Montreal's English-speaking businessmen prepared a French-speaking proletariat for them. Gradually the ethnic balance of the city shifted toward the French as French Canada itself shifted from a rural and conservative society to an urban society with typically North American objectives.

Before all this changed, a young teacher, Hugh MacLennan, arrived in the city from the Maritimes and described it with bleak but indelible accuracy in one of his early works as a community of *Two Solitudes*. There were many solitudes in Montreal, including the Jewish world that still nourishes the literary genius of Mordecai Richler, but none were afflicted with a modern sense of guilt about their isolation from one another. Each contained a rich life within itself, small enough to be an identifiable community but also taking pride in the achievements of the metropolis. As Richler still discovers universal stories in the Jewish ghetto of Montreal, Mavis Gallant in Paris explores English-speaking Montreal of the same period in stories that also attract an international audience.

It was a world in the process of destroying itself. From a high point in the nineteenth century, when Irish immigrants flooded into the city, the English diminished in relation to the French. As a minority, they gradually lost the trappings of political power but, for a time, retained its substance. They dominated the business life of the city and retained a privileged position for themselves and their institutions.

In the sixties, French-speaking Montrealers were no longer content to have their progress depend on the goodwill of their English-speaking neighbours. They embarked on the conquest of Montreal.

By this time, the two communities were hopelessly out of touch with one another. The English couldn't translate the political vocabulary that seemed to emerge suddenly on the other side. It was difficult enough for many French-speaking Montrealers to think of themselves as "white niggers of America" and to regard their English-speaking neighbours as "Rhodesians"; for most of the English, it required an effort of sympathetic imagination that was far beyond their capacity. As the rhetoric became more and more strident, the original paternalistic benevolence of the English hardened into a dogged and uncomprehending resentment, at least among those who stayed.

At the outset of the struggle, the English were abandoned by many of their leaders. While businessmen started to move capital and jobs out of the city, the most respected spokesmen for the English community tried to take an open-minded and progressive attitude toward the changes. Many of them joined with French-speaking intellectuals in a critical examination of the privileges enjoyed by the English. Optimists on both sides preached that mutual development was possible, that the French could progress rapidly without sudden or significant adverse effects on the English.

Perhaps this innocent spirit of goodwill helped to calm the English minority in this early stage, but it was as unrealistic as the less sophisticated call to the barricades that was heard from time to time on open-line radio shows. The French were determined to have a bigger share of the community's assets and the English could do nothing about this, apart from trying to see developments as clearly as possible and adapting to them pragmatically.

If the economy of the city had been expanding at this time, it might have been possible for the English to hold their own while the French took the lion's share of the new growth. In fact, the city was in a period of relative decline as the economic centre of Canada moved west. Political conflict accelerated this descent. Eventually it became clear that gains by the French would be made, to some extent, at the expense of the English. This was soon noticed in such vital institutions as schools and hospitals.

The English of Quebec also received a hard lesson in Canadian regionalism. No one in the rest of the country cared what happened to them. Canadians elsewhere still resented the economic dominance of St. James Street and perhaps were secretly delighted at this humbling of the high and mighty. They were also too occupied in making their own bargains with the political demands of Quebec to spare much thought for the millionaires of Westmount. In a fragmented country such as ours, there was no ability outside of Quebec to discriminate between Westmount and the fate of the vast majority of English-speaking Montrealers who lived in the middle-class and working-class districts of the city below the hill. They were simply written off by everyone.

If anyone in this country has reason to complain about developments in the past twenty years, it is this English-speaking population of Quebec, the ones who stayed by choice or by necessity. They saw their business activities curtailed, their community institutions starved for funds, and the value of their homes decline. Without exaggerating the extent of their sacrifices, believe me, they have been real; and as someone raised in that community and aware of its efforts to adapt, I have had little patience at times with my English-speaking compatriots in other cities who have complained loudly about the inconvenience and expense of introducing French-language television stations or providing French-language courts and other services for their own minorities.

Changes in Montreal were barely underway in the early sixties when the bombs started to explode. In the perspective of international terrorism, the violence in Quebec in the sixties was almost insignificant, but it came as a shock to Canadians who long ago had forgotten their abortive nineteenth-century rebellions in Lower and Upper Canada. It was traumatic for English-speaking Montrealers whose image of a city based essentially on goodwill and co-operation blew up in their faces. The bombs and their random victims forced Montrealers to appreciate the deep antagonisms between English and French in Quebec. It wasn't only the bombs and the Marxist propaganda that accompanied them; these were part of the sixties in many countries. It was the persistence of the terrorism throughout the sixties – the time that it took for many

French-speaking Québécois to make up their minds about it. The English-speaking community was forced to realize that terrorism, for a time, was a means of expression tolerated if not endorsed by many of their French-speaking neighbours. That inescapable truth had an immediate and profoundly depressing effect on the entire city.

It was desperately hard for Canadians to accept that someone hated them deeply enough to want to kill them.

English-speaking Quebecers also came to understand that the terrorism accomplished its objectives, at least up to the October Crisis of 1970. Other Canadians now paid attention. The violence put Quebec on the world map. How many political changes would have occurred without this extreme expression of Quebec nationalism will never be known, but certainly not as many nor as quickly. Violence in Quebec in the sixties was a catalyst, and perhaps a necessity.

Many French-speaking Quebecers in the 1960's were convinced of that. Many of us listened to them, read about them, studied their manifestos, puzzled over their books and magazines. The means they advocated were abhorrent, yet their insights were often devastating. Theirs was a narrow, but piercing, perspective. The inequalities and injustices they opposed with their lives were part of the fabric of our own. We came to understand we would have to do violence to our own view of ourselves if there was to be any hope of peaceful change.

During the eight years of sporadic terrorism in Montreal, French and English asked themselves if this were the true image of their city: another Belfast. It was so close in many respects that it took a long time to discover where the differences lay.

The terrorists themselves concluded this part of our education by escalating the violence in October, 1970, kidnapping a British diplomat and murdering a Quebec cabinet minister. The reaction in Quebec was so immediate and universal that violence was instantly outmoded as a political weapon. That liberated us to explore other instruments with the deeper understanding of ourselves that we had gained under fire.

After 1970, everyone accepted the inevitability of change. No one any longer believed that it was going to be easy.

Change was expressed politically by the language laws enacted by the Liberal government of Robert Bourassa and the Parti Québécois government of René Lévesque. The laws were designed to ensure the numerical supremacy of the French in Montreal and their rise to a dominant position in the economic life of the city. By 1970, most English-speaking Canadians in Quebec and the rest of the country had come to regard these developments as inevitable. Still, they found it difficult to accept the language laws because they seemed to be a form of overkill based on dubious statistics and inspired partly by vengeance.

The main intent of the language laws was the conquest of Montreal, a city that had never belonged to the French-speaking majority in the province. I can remember René Lévesque telling me, years ago, about the shock of his first exposure to Montreal as a new arrival from the Gaspé, when he discovered that the metropolis of Quebec was, at heart, an English-speaking city. English was heard everywhere but in the poorer districts of the east end. The city even looked English with its streets named after British colonial heroes and Anglican bishops and dominated by advertising for American products.

It wasn't hard to imagine this state of affairs continuing as the birth rate of French-speaking Québécois dropped sharply and immigrants flooded into the city. Population studies in the sixties showed that 80 per cent of the new arrivals joined the English-speaking community and sent their numerous children to English-language schools. These trends were projected at that time in forecasts warning that 40 per cent of the city's population might be English-speaking by the end of the century. From the rest of Canada, at the same time, there was indisputable evidence that the use of French was declining. It was estimated that the proportion of Francophones in the national population might drop from 27 per cent in 1971 to 20 per cent by the year 2000.

French-speaking Québécois felt that they faced the prospect of losing political influence nationally at the same time as English-speaking Montrealers consolidated their authority over the metropolis that dominated the commercial and intellectual life of Quebec. This assessment of the future convinced a majority of Québécois that it was time for drastic action. They supported moves by Quebec governments to remove some language privileges that English-speaking Montrealers had come to regard as traditional rights.

Many of these rights had never been shared by French-speaking minorities outside Quebec, in theory or in practice. That weakened the desire or ability of other Canadians to protest the sudden change of custom in Quebec, despite the fact that, in its original form, the 1977 legislation would have classified them as aliens for school purposes if they had tried to emigrate to Quebec.

Immigrants were the main target of these changes. They lost the freedom to send their children to schools of their choice, English or French. After much discussion in Quebec's National Assembly, new arrivals from other provinces were given the special privilege of enrolling their children in English-language schools for a limited number of years.

The English minority fought these changes with every weapon at its disposal. It was a question of survival. Without the reinforcement of thousands of immigrants every year, its school systems would deteriorate, its universities would be endangered, its news media would become weaker, its cultural institutions would start to die, and the entire community would begin a long retreat into relative insignificance. The issue was clear to everyone in Quebec.

The language laws also provided for regulation of business language in the city. Advertising had to be predominantly French. The language of work must be increasingly French. Systems of bureaucratic inspection and control were designed, which created predictable absurdities such as ordering Protestant churches to produce bilingual bulletins for their congregations. Even after some of the bureaucratic excesses were controlled, the "francization" program remained cumbersome and costly.

As the laws were being enacted, there were more and more doubts about their practical necessity. All the dire population predictions of the 1960's had been based on the assumption that current trends would continue in a straight line. In a province as volatile as Quebec at that time, that was unlikely. Even as the Quebec demographers were making their projections, the English were streaming out of Quebec toward Ontario and the western provinces. Head offices moved toward greener commercial fields. Economic and political developments were transforming Montreal from a national centre of commerce and finance into a regional metropolis serving Quebec. This was reflected in the structure of many businesses. It made economic and political sense in the 1960's for many corporations to centre their Canadian operations in Toronto or perhaps even further west while their Montreal offices became regional headquarters operating in French and staffed by French-speaking Québécois.

In the 1960's, the inferior position of French as a business language had been clearly defined. A survey of forty-one large Canadian companies in 1964 showed that Francophones represented only 15 per cent of senior management personnel. But there were signs of change in the early 1970's. A breakdown of Statistics Canada figures for 1971 showed that Francophones made up only 53.4 per cent of business managers in Quebec over sixty years of age but 73.3 per cent of those in the 20-29 age group. Another study of changes in Quebec's management group from 1971 to 1978 showed that the proportion of Francophones had increased from 68 to 75 per cent, reflecting a gain of about 20,000 senior positions for Francophones and a loss of about 8,000 for Anglophones. Changes as substantial as this occur over a long period of time for a variety of reasons. In this case, the pattern of change was set before the language legislation came into effect.

The new laws were passed primarily because the economic relationship of English and French in Montreal not only had to change, but had to be seen to be changing. Every Quebec government since 1960 has had to enact legislation or regulations to protect the French language. The current "federalist" opposition in Quebec under Liberal Leader Claude Ryan may allow Montreal's dwindling stream of new immigrants to send their children to English-language schools, if it comes to power, but it won't dismantle the program to enforce the use of French as the main language of commerce.

Language laws have been so important to a series of Quebec governments that they have been willing to suffer economic loss and court ridicule to enforce them. A study published this year by the C.D. Howe Research Institute in Montreal estimated that the 1977 *Charter of the French Language* cost Quebec about 14,000 jobs, almost the annual number of jobs created in the province. In addition to this economic price, Quebec paid dearly in terms of its relations with the rest of Canada. Eliminating English advertising signs by legislation appeared absurd and petty to many Canadians in other provinces who failed to perceive that it symbolized a decisive change in the character of the city, the province, and the whole nation.

It was a question of pride for Québécois. For several centuries, they had existed in an inferior position to the English in their own province. By 1960, they were ready not only to take charge of their own future but to settle some old scores. It was the turn of the English in Quebec to complain about discrimination.

Quebec politicians didn't want to hear that the language laws were redundant, that perhaps they were firing all their heavy artillery at an enemy who already was on the run. They needed to use the power they now had and to see a few bodies on the battlefield.

The same sense of pride explained the city's commitment to the Olympic Games in 1976 and its continued attachment to a Mayor who blatantly mishandled the planning and organization of the Games. Jean Drapeau had a great deal to learn about monumental architecture and construction, but no one could teach him anything about the psychology of his citizens. The Olympic Games, like Expo 67, like the conflict over language, gave French-speaking Montrealers a sense of pride and purpose at a time when these were invaluable to the city.

The bitter struggle is now over. Although the English of Montreal will remain an important minority, the city is irrevocably French. It is also poorer, having been displaced by Calgary as the most important financial centre after Toronto. But it has confronted the antagonisms between English and French, admitted the existence of deep hatreds, adjusted to violence, accepted the inevitability of change, and survived.

The city looks battered these days but better, not as cheerless as it was in the early seventies. The English who weren't able to tolerate the changes have moved out, leaving behind a resourceful and increasingly bilingual community of Anglo-Quebecers who consciously strive for a positive response to the majority. Contacts between English and French are more frequent and more straightforward. Both groups have been influenced by the growing conservatism of North American society and this makes it easier to concentrate less on political squabbling and more on economic development. Even the damaged economy of the city, with its low rents and depressed housing prices, is being advertised to prospective investors as a positive feature.

The economic and social struggle between English and French in Montreal was at the heart of the "Quebec problem" that has obsessed us nationally for the past two decades. Montreal had to become essentially a French-speaking city before French and English Quebecers could discuss realistically the position of Quebec within Confederation.

10.
Quebec and Alberta:
The State of the East and
the Empire of the West

In the past two decades, Quebec has acquired all the virtues, defects, and paraphernalia of modern North American society. It has a middle-class where none existed before. Many of its members work for the government in a bureaucracy that is capable of handling the affairs of an independent country and would, in an instant, if it had the chance. It has a modern system of schools where teachers, zealous in the defence of their rights, produce students who seem to have little concept of their obligations to society. Despite inflation and unemployment and the burdens of government, it appears to be a prosperous and comfortable society indistinguishable at first glance from Canadian society elsewhere.

If it weren't for differences of language, Québécois would have everything in common with other Canadians, which of course is like saying that only pigmentation of the skin gives the United States a racial problem. Language is almost as indelible as skin colour and under pressure to erase it, it becomes almost as durable. No one can take blackness away from the blacks – there's a certain security in that – but people have lost languages. The possibility of that, with its consequent loss of identity, is so terrifying to most communities that they will go almost to any lengths to preserve their own language.

But more than language separated Québécois and other Canadians only a generation ago. Quebec was Roman Catholic; English was the language of Protestantism. Quebecers were still close to farm and village. They were encouraged to believe that they were a people chosen by God to follow a higher path, above a pagan, materialistic world. Nothing of this special vocation is left. The immediate concerns of French-speaking Québécois are identical with those of Torontonians or Calgarians. The rationale for accepting a lower standard of living and a subservient economic role has disappeared. For better or worse, we all now are closer to one another. We expect the same things from life.

As Quebec society became less distinctive in some respects, Quebec politically became more different. Quebec as a bilingual province where the English made up in money what they lacked in manpower had adhered to the ideal Canadian pattern more closely than most other provinces. As an increasingly unilingual province, it was a new entity. Its attitude toward the rest of the country changed.

Under the conservative leadership of Premier Maurice Duplessis, Quebec had maintained a defensive and negative role in the federation. It had tried to exercise a veto over national decisions, and when that failed it had retreated into impregnable constitutional positions. It had resisted change almost at any cost.

Under Duplessis, Quebec prospered, education expanded, and new ideas began to circulate despite his authoritarian rule. The generation of Québécois who have dominated Ottawa and Quebec in our own time were formed, in a sense, by Duplessis. Their best ideas about human society and Canada's political structure were inspired by their opposition to his reactionary and corrupt regime.

Public opinion is "the opinion of those who are against us," said Duplessis. It came into its own after his death in 1959. Many Quebecers felt they had regained their homeland. They were determined to transform it from a quaint backwater into a model North American society.

Those early days of the Quiet Revolution were frantic with activity, effervescent with ideas, and glowing with optimism. Québécois stated their determination to become masters of their own destiny. They explored the world beyond their borders with insatiable curiosity, reaching out in particular to France and her former colonies to establish Quebec as a member of the international French-speaking community.

It was a time of bewildering change. The Catholic Church was dispatched into the background with an efficiency that communist regimes would have envied. Labour unions had to shift overnight from opposing the government to collaborating with it. Bureaucrats tried to use television in the remote Gaspé to turn farmers and fishermen into political activists. They dreamed of transforming their society by pushing buttons in Quebec City. Utopia was just around the corner.

The first separatists at this time were as simple and as lovable as St.

Francis. The television producers of English-speaking Canada filled their studios with them, encouraged them to talk of Quebec embassies, armies, dollars, and dreadnoughts. It was pure entertainment for many Canadians, watching these bearded eccentric revolutionaries shake their fists at the cameras like angry Hobbits. These early separatists rarely noticed the skepticism of English Canada, so persuaded were they of the rightness of their cause and the inevitability of victory. Their ideal of independence was pure. Most of them, today, cannot forgive René Lévesque and his colleagues for ruining separatism by trying to put it into a viable political platform.

Separatism has never seemed closer than it did in those first years. In the beginning, there was only the dream of independence and the illusion that believing in it would be enough to make it happen. Many people in Quebec began to think it was inevitable. Only as the idea took political shape, ultimately in the Parti Québécois, did the obstacles become tangible.

Separatism was a reality in those years in the sense that Canadians in Quebec and in the other provinces inhabited different worlds. Nothing in English Canada corresponded to the changes that were occurring in Quebec. Society in English Canada matured more slowly, almost imperceptibly, while Quebec's headlong rush into the future carried it farther and farther away from the rest of the country.

In other provinces, they asked, "What does Quebec want?" It would have been easier to determine what it didn't want. It asked for everything at once – more independence and more money from Canada, more business development and more socialist policies, more democracy and bigger limousines for cabinet ministers. It was contradictory, but that alone didn't make Quebec incomprehensible elsewhere in Canada. The main obstacle to understanding Quebec was the old picture of Quebec society that took years to fade from the minds of Canadians.

When we began to see Québécois as being remarkably like ourselves, we no longer wondered what they wanted. They wanted what we already had economically and, politically, what many of us had dreamed about: freedom and independence.

After the bombings of the 1960's, when the dust had settled, Quebecers set out collectively to discover how far they could go on the road to independence. By this time they were led by René Lévesque, whose political strength lay partly in the limited nature of his objective.

No one seems to know exactly when Lévesque became a separatist.

He has assigned different dates on various occasions to this momentous conversion, perhaps because it never actually occurred. Lévesque has always been determined to push the idea of Quebec independence, and his own political career, as far as he could but no further. His pragmatic approach to the idea of independence is shared by the vast majority of Québécois, and because of that they have trusted him. I once referred to Lévesque as "a Canadian in search of a country." The quest has lasted now for twenty years, affecting every aspect of our political life. It came within sight of the end, at least for Lévesque, at least for this generation, in the 1980 referendum. It remains to be seen where and how it will come to rest.

The idea of independence started to lose momentum after the 1972 Quebec election when the Parti Québécois realized it was an electoral liability. The referendum was adopted as a means of removing it from the next Quebec election. As a tactical device, it was brilliant; as a means of achieving independence by stages, it was fraudulent. The election of a Parti Québécois government in 1976 shocked the rest of Canada into believing briefly that the separatists had gained control of Quebec. They were in control of the government, it was true, but only by becoming federalists at least for a time. They had won only by promising to keep Quebec in Confederation unless otherwise instructed in a second referendum.

The referendum in 1980 confirmed Quebec's adherence to the idea of Canada. Conceived as a desperate electoral strategy by the Parti Québécois, it was transformed by all Quebecers into an impressive affirmation of Canadian nationhood in a province where that was least expected.

Some feared that Canada would go to sleep after the Quebec referendum. They forgot that the other Canadian provinces had woken up in the meantime. Demands for change were now being heard everywhere in the country, particularly in the West. Quebec as a source of concern had given way to Alberta.

When separatism first became a force in Quebec, it was almost impossible to communicate what was happening in Quebec to the rest of the country. Many of us tried because we believed, as a matter of faith, that better communication would solve most of the problems, that all we had to do was understand Quebec's objectives in order to negotiate them sensibly. Despite my own belief in the power of the word, printed and electronic, I began to wonder after a time if all the activity made much difference under the circumstances. I was part of the process that inundated English-speaking Canada with newspaper columns, magazine articles, and television documentaries about Quebec, but when I went to western Canada people still complained about a lack of information. "What does Quebec want?" they would say. It wasn't that they didn't want to understand. They couldn't. Their own experience of Canada had left them blind and deaf to the experience that Quebecers were undergoing.

During this time, English-speaking Canadians were happy with things as they were, more or less, particularly in Ontario and western Canada. We didn't see any need for drastic political changes. We listened with polite indifference to Quebec most of the time. If the pressure for change increased, we became irritable. We had the feeling that someone was trying to push something down our throats— bilingualism, biculturalism, special status, sovereignty-association—and we weren't hungry. It made us gag.

Quebec and the rest of Canada were out of synchronization. Changes in Quebec had accelerated because of conditions there. The Quiet Revolution had little to do with the rest of Canada. It was only when changes began to occur in the rest of Canada, for equally indigenous reasons, and when Quebec slowed down a little, that the two communities found themselves moving at the same speed. Issues suddenly came into focus. Links could be established.

Changes in the rest of the country occurred for different reasons. Economic development had much to do with it. That mystified many Québécois as much as their concern about language had puzzled the West. They couldn't understand why rich Albertans were complaining. With all that money and with no grievances about language or culture, Alberta looked like paradise to many people in Quebec.

Now they are beginning to detect more than oil in Alberta. They can identify pride, a commodity that all Quebecers can recognize and understand. It is dawning on Québécois that the rest of Canada is not as uniform as they once had thought. Language is not the only thing that divides Canadians. Quebec is not the only region with its own history and its own way of interpreting our national history.

Alberta is only seventy-five years old, but it has had more than enough time, in this fragmented nation, to develop its own set of grievances against the rest of us. As every Québécois has a personal story about mistreatment by the English, older residents of Alberta remember how they were treated by central Canada when the province didn't have enough water to grow wheat, before the oil started to flow. The trust companies of eastern Canada squeezed Peter Lougheed's own family during the Depression and the Premier is said never to have forgotten. Albertans can distrust Toronto and hate Ottawa with an intensity that would startle many Québécois.

At times, western separatism seems more aggressive and uncompromising than the Quebec variety. From the days when Premier Jean Lesage tried hopelessly to explain Quebec to western audiences in the 1960's, Quebec has tried to communicate with the rest of Canada. Premier Lévesque is almost as familiar to audiences outside Quebec as he is to his own constituents. Alberta strikes an attitude that is more independent, in practice. Justifications for Alberta positions are rarely considered necessary. The case for the West is presented to the rest of the country as if it were self-explanatory.

This Alberta attitude is not only for public display, part of the dramatics of federal-provincial negotiations that many Quebec leaders have learned to use effectively. It continues into private federal-provincial meetings. In his book, *Discipline of Power*, about the 1979 Conservative interregnum in Ottawa, Jeffrey Simpson of *The Globe and Mail* paints a detailed picture of Lougheed's attitude toward a Prime Minister.

"The meeting was a disaster," he wrote, describing a negotiating session between the Alberta Premier, Prime Minister Clark, and senior members of their two cabinets in Montreal on Thanksgiving Day, 1979. "Lougheed was at his cantankerous worst, giving the Prime Minister and his ministers a lecture on everything that Alberta was doing for Canada. With scarcely an exchange of pleasantries, Lougheed laid down the Alberta position, more or less on a take-it-or-leave-it basis." When Clark and his ministers asked for time to consider the Alberta proposal, Lougheed, "with scarcely a parting word, gathered up his papers and stomped out of the meeting."

Clark had once worked for Lougheed. The Alberta Premier had little personal respect for him. Still, the picture of the leader of one of our ten provinces trying to dictate to the federal government – playing the part of the "Ayatollah," as Clark's Finance Minister, John Crosbie, used to say – turns the accepted concept of our confederation upside-down.

According to Simpson, Lougheed was talking in November, 1979, about splitting his provincial Conservative Party from the federal party. This threat to create a distinctive Alberta party, as Premier Duplessis more than forty years earlier had founded the Union Nationale in Quebec, was the biggest step toward the concept of political separatism that western Canada had yet seen. This was more than the separatist ramblings of a handful of western dissidents on the fringes of the political system, the voices we had heard in the 1960's, an echo of the furore in Quebec. Lougheed's threat was an indigenous Albertan response to specific pressure from outside the province. It had to be taken seriously.

All of us have become so used to thinking of Quebec or French as the disruptive element in Confederation, particularly in Quebec and Ontario, that it takes time to understand that oil can play the same role. "Petroleum has come to symbolize competing visions of Canada," stated *The Globe and Mail* in September, 1980. Only a few years earlier, the subject of the same sentence would have been "bilingualism."

"Provincial ownership of resources is one of the fundamental cornerstones of Confederation," Premier Lougheed stated in 1979, as categorically as Quebec premiers in recent decades have defended their jurisdiction over education, language, and culture. "Petrodollars, not constitutional lawyers, are rewriting our federal system," warned Ontario Treasurer Frank Miller in 1979. "Without a referendum or a mandate, these money flows are quickly destroying the authority of our federal government to pursue its historic responsibilities."

In Quebec, the force for change was internal. Rapid economic and social changes in Quebec made a new arrangement with the rest of Canada essential. The new Quebec could not be accommodated in the old Confederation. Changes in Alberta and the other western provinces have been triggered by events outside Canada. Global resource shortages and higher international prices for oil and other resources have vastly increased the wealth generated within Alberta, and, to a lesser extent, Saskatchewan and British Columbia. Alberta now earns about $4 billion annually from the sale of oil and gas, up from $500 million in 1973. In 1980, the province's Heritage Fund contained more than $6 billion. Saskatchewan has started a similar fund for accumulated oil, gas, and potash revenues. Calgary and Edmonton will soon be cities of a million people each. The price of houses in these cities and Vancouver now bears the same relation to Toronto prices as Toronto prices bore to Montreal's in the past decade.

People have moved toward the money. In 1979, Ontario lost an estimated 30,000 people and $3 billion in business investment to western Canada. The West's population is now larger than Quebec's for the first time since Confederation. Before the end of the century, the economic output of the West is expected to exceed Ontario's. Ten years ago, it was only 60 per cent of Ontario's output.

Like Quebec, the western provinces are frightened by doomsday scenarios of the future. Québécois have worried about their language disappearing. Westerners worry about the depletion of their oil and gas reserves. Even as the billions accumulate, Alberta's oil production heads into a gradual decline. The need to defend its resources is seen as a question of survival, as language is in Quebec.

Wealthier economies in the western provinces and a healthier society in Quebec are good developments in themselves, but they contribute to the whole country only if they are integrated in a national pattern.

In the spring of 1980, the C.D. Howe Research Institute in Montreal warned that our economy is "in a process of disintegration" with "all the strong provinces turning their backs on nation-building and trying to create their own balanced, self-contained, little economies." The Institute said that this process was accelerating, and predicted that within five or ten years Manitoba and the Maritimes might be the only provinces interested in defending an integrated national economy.

The author of the Institute's study was Caroline Pestiau, a Quebec economist who had set out after the 1976 Quebec election to investigate the Ottawa-Quebec problem. She discovered, as she told a newspaper interviewer, that "René Lévesque's separatism is only the catalyst that set off the process of disintegration."

The "Quebec problem" has now been joined by the "Alberta problem" and by related problems in all other provinces. This brings us closer to dissolution as a nation and, paradoxically, offers us the first real prospect of change. As long as our national problem seemed to originate within Quebec, it was hard to convince many of us that it was our problem. The rest of the country felt it was being pressured to accommodate changes in only one province. All the demands were coming from Quebec. The rest of Canada was expected to make all the concessions.

Now the centre of discontent has moved westward. The practical dangers of a high level of discontent in Alberta have almost made us forget temporarily about Quebec. Newfoundland, hungry for the offshore oil revenues that seem to lie just over the horizon, has allied itself with Alberta's struggle for control of resources. No one can argue any longer that our problems are confined to a single province. They are national in scope, creating a truly national sense of concern, which, hopefully, can lead to national solutions. We can now see Quebec not as the beginning of all our problems but as part of the solution, perhaps the key.

The objectives of Alberta and Quebec seem diametrically opposed – a greater degree of economic sovereignty in the West, of political sovereignty in the East – but the motives are not all that different. "Quebecers have a desire to be masters in their own house," said Premier Lougheed after the 1976 election victory of the Parti Québécois. "I have an empathy with that feeling." That shared sense of pride can be the start of mutual understanding and eventual compromise.

The specific objectives of the provinces also are closely related. The Quebec problem, as we have discovered, is a basic element of our paralysis in the face of major national challenges, including the task of properly utilizing our energy resources for the common good. If it has interfered with our efforts to find a national solution to our energy problems, it stands to reason that the road to accommodation with Alberta leads through Quebec.

Everyone isn't going to get everything they want. Concessions will be possible if we can see that they are shared by many. If Albertans find aspects of political sovereignty repugnant, if they support the federal government's assertion of its political sovereignty, perhaps this will make it easier for them to accept limits on their economic sovereignty. If these limits are supported by Québécois for their own reasons, the case for maintaining a strong political federation becomes more convincing to Quebec.

Our problems are now so severe and so universal that these interconnections appear everywhere. Paradoxically, the more widespread our problems become, the easier it is for us to see our dependence on one another. Tampering with one aspect alone or with one region, as the Quebec separatists would do, seems more and more impractical. We will have to solve our problems together.

We've come a long way from the early days of separatism in Quebec when it seemed outlandish to think of the disintegration of Canada. Now it seems all too imminent, but we also are beginning to understand that the original threat of a Québec Libre has transformed itself, over the years, into the promise of a truly liberated Canada.

If that promise is going to be realized, it will require political leadership of the highest order – visionary, courageous, intuitive, and decisive. By a series of political accidents, the only contemporary leader who conceivably could achieve this has returned to power at this time. Pierre Trudeau finds himself Prime Minister again during the brief period when real change is possible. Our future and his are now inextricably linked.

11.
Run, Pierre, Run

At the end of 1979, Pierre Trudeau announced his retirement from politics. He had been defeated earlier that year by a younger and, in many respects, less competent politician. The vote, according to the polls, had been against Trudeau rather than in favour of Joe Clark. As Leader of the Opposition in Parliament, Trudeau had been lazy, bored, and ineffective. It seemed that he had nothing more to contribute.

Within a few months, Trudeau was Prime Minister again. Victory seemed to bring new energy and purpose. A few more months and he was focusing his efforts and our attention on a task that had baffled him for fifteen years and frustrated Canadian politicians for more than fifty: reforming the constitution and bringing it home. He was within sight of an achievement that would ensure his place in Canadian history.

This sequence of events was so improbable that it bordered on the miraculous. Yet it was only what many Canadians expected of Trudeau, or feared from him – *The Northern Magus*, as Richard Gwyn calls him in his recent critical biography. His whole career has had a magical, superhuman quality, from the "Trudeaumania" of 1968 through his near-defeat in 1972, his political resurrection in 1974, his apparently conclusive defeat in 1979, and his return to office in 1980.

Destiny or accident, Trudeau's fourth term as Prime Minister coincides with a brief moment in our history when political conditions and public attitudes may permit patriation and reform of the constitution. The most recent nationalist cycle in Quebec has expressed itself in the 1980 referendum. Western Canada reflects Quebec demands for change, increasing the possibility of compromise if not reconciliation. Public opinion polls show that Canadians generally support bringing home the constitution.

Conditions have never been more favourable for a decisive move. If it is going to happen in our generation, it will happen within a short time, certainly within the limited time remaining to Trudeau as our Prime Minister. No matter what we think of him or how we feel about him, he is the only one who can do it. No one has ever been better equipped or prepared for this task. No one, also, has had more awesome handicaps. He will have to change if the country is to accept change, and this personal renewal will be as difficult as the political because his weaknesses are intimately related to his strengths.

He is, first of all, from Quebec, from a particular period in Quebec history when it required intellectual and physical courage to be a federalist. He discovered federalism as a source of freedom in the narrow and authoritarian world of Quebec politics controlled by Premier Maurice Duplessis. To be a federalist in Quebec in the 1950's was to fight underground for freedoms that could be defended with absolute conviction – freedom of religion, freedom of expression in the press and universities, and the free association of workers in labour unions. English and French in Quebec fought alongside one another in this struggle. It transcended the old divisions of their society.

Trudeau carried the genes of both communities within himself, as do millions of Canadians. To advocate division has always seemed to him schizophrenic: Why should he set one part of himself against the other? Deny one part to advance the other? He has always been proud of the distinctive features of his own character that could be labelled Trudeau or Elliott. He has remembered his Scottish-Canadian grandfather: "a very mobile face, quite pockmarked . . . very lively . . . a man who knows how to do everything. . . . " His French-Canadian grandmother was "always dressed in black . . . hair pulled back and gathered behind her head . . . a very lined face . . . very religious. . . . " To his father, Charlie Trudeau, he has attributed his own passion for "order and discipline." From Grace Elliott, his mother, he believes that he inherited "freedom and fantasy." But he also remembers his father, a successful businessman, as being witty and more exuberant than himself.

This is a favourite human game, trying to identify the characteristics and features of our ancestors in ourselves, and Pierre Trudeau has enjoyed playing it in many interviews. The essential duality of the Canadian experience is reflected in his most intimate memories and thoughts of himself.

He also knows the loneliness and pride of the mongrel whose pedigree is not purebred. As a young man, he deliberately gave prominence to the Elliott name to flaunt his mixed parentage before other students who boasted of their Québécois ancestry. Many of us whose names and family languages have been jumbled over the centuries to produce strange hybrids also have felt this sense of exclusion at times and have shared Trudeau's pride in the "new nationality" D'Arcy McGee proclaimed but which we have yet to achieve fully. Pierre Trudeau's attempts to define this nationality in political terms, one of the consistent objectives of his career, are inspired by his understanding of himself.

A politician who feels such a close identity with his country draws immense power from it. His experience is the opposite of the modern political leader whose views are fashioned to correspond to the findings of public opinion polls. The hallmark of the "customized" leader is the slogan that seeks to express a public mood rather than a principle of government. These slogans rarely can be translated into effective policies.

Trudeau's party has used slogans, but Trudeau himself has always had the ability to express his beliefs in words that sound original and fresh. They sound convincing because they transmit his convictions.

In contrast, Joe Clark's concept of Canada as a "community of communities" was ineffective. Although it was related to his own upbringing in western Canada, it seemed to lack both intellectual depth and emotional commitment. Clark himself seemed to have little idea of its meaning when he was elected Prime Minister. During his brief term in office, his government was unable to use the slogan as the framework of a recognizable national policy.

Trudeau, when he first became Prime Minister, had a clear idea of what he wanted to do. His concept of Canada was formed long before he entered politics and it has remained clearly in focus ever since. One of his oldest friends and colleagues, Gérard Pelletier, recalled that during their student days Trudeau possessed "a fund of knowledge on Canada." He would organize discussions on the Canadian constitution and quote at length from speeches by Sir John A. Macdonald.

Trudeau arrived in the House of Commons in 1965 as an academic authority on constitutional law. Reform of the constitution was one of his first assignments as Justice Minister under Prime Minister Pearson. Years earlier, writing in *Cité Libre*, the small magazine he had founded with Pelletier and others, Trudeau had defined his main constitutional objective: " . . . a declaration of rights entrenched in the constitution which would be binding on all Canadians and on all our governments. . . . that would enable us to agree on basic principles and lead us even, I think, to a formula for amending the constitution, which in turn would enable us to repatriate the constitution." In his first constitutional proposal as Justice Minister in 1967, he repeated these objectives. Change would commence with entrenching a bill of rights binding on the federal and provincial governments. This remains his approach toward reform and patriation of the constitution.

At a televised federal-provincial conference in 1968, Trudeau's clash with Quebec Premier Daniel Johnson over special constitutional status for Quebec and the need for a constitutional bill of rights presented him to many Canadians, for the first time, as a possible national leader. In 1968, Trudeau hoped for conclusive negotiations with Quebec. "No more of this open-ended negotiation," he said in a television interview. "This is the idea of Munich. It may be we need a showdown . . . ." Munich, in this case, has lasted for more than twelve years.

Trudeau's first and most frustrating attempt to bring home the constitution occupied his energies from 1968 to 1971 and seemed to be crowned with success at the concluding conference in Victoria. All the provinces appeared to agree on a formula for amending the constitution after patriation. The agreement evaporated when Quebec Premier Robert Bourassa returned home to encounter a solid wall of resistance in his own province led by such influential figures as Claude Ryan, now the leader of the Quebec Liberals, who was then director and chief editorialist of the Montreal daily *Le Devoir*. A second attempt from 1976 to 1979 failed utterly, despite concessions by Ottawa that probably would have ensured success had they been offered in 1971. The conclusive rejection by Canadians seemed to occur in the 1979 election, when the Prime Minister made constitutional reform one of the main elements of his disastrous campaign.

In his most important speech in the final days of the 1979 campaign, before an audience of 20,000 in Toronto's Maple Leaf Gardens, Trudeau promised that a new Liberal government would recall Parliament immediately to approve a resolution to patriate the constitution. This would be followed by a year of meetings with the premiers to draft a new constitution. If the Premiers were unable to reach agreement with Ottawa, "We will consult the people of Canada in a national referendum. We will have a Canadian constitution, made by Canadians for Canadians, and we will do it together." Three days before the election, Trudeau said: "Either we will have one strong country, or we will have a country of ten independent principalities. Let us all bring it all together in one gigantic act of national will."

Trudeau won 40 per cent of the vote to Clark's 36 per cent but lost the election. Canadians had other things on their minds than the constitution. They seemed determined to humble Trudeau and the Liberals as they had done in 1972. If the election did represent an act of national will, it was to teach the Prime Minister a lesson. In this setting, his call for reform of the constitution looked like a desperate manoeuvre to shield him from disaster.

As Prime Minister, Joe Clark showed no interest in resurrecting what seemed to be a dead issue. Trudeau paid almost no attention to the constitution in his 1980 campaign while he concentrated on attacking the Tories' record in office. As soon as he returned to power, it again became a priority. By the spring of 1980, it had emerged as the main objective of the new Trudeau government, and in June the First Ministers met to open a new round of negotiations.

Federal and provincial ministers were occupied throughout the summer in discussing a dozen areas of constitutional reform defined by the Prime Minister and the premiers. When the First Ministers met again in September, they were under the threat of unilateral action by Trudeau, who had promised before the meeting that he would bring home the constitution before the end of the year.

Canadians seemed ready to listen to him this time. A Gallup poll taken in July showed that 78 per cent of those polled agreed that "Canada should have its own constitution, written and adopted by Canadians, rather than continuing to use the British North America Act of 1867." Support for this was highest in the four western provinces, where Trudeau was weakest politically. There was an even higher degree of support – 81 per cent – for the proposition that "where numbers warrant, French minorities outside of Quebec and English minorities inside of Quebec, be guaranteed the right to education in their own language." Nine out of ten respondents agreed that the constitution should guarantee basic human rights to all Canadians.

Perhaps the message of Trudeau's 1979 campaign had been heard after all. Perhaps, in what appeared to be his final term as Prime Minister, Canadians were prepared to grant him the objective that had eluded him for fifteen years. Trudeau seemed determined to seize the opportunity and to bring the long, sporadic process of constitutional change to a conclusion. With his academic background, his mastery of the issues, his familiarity with the premiers, and his ability to dominate them at federal-provincial conferences, he seemed to be in a unique position to succeed, despite the hurdles that still lay ahead. But the personal shortcomings that contributed to failures in the past are still there. Every one of his strengths in this final struggle seems to have a negative aspect.

His deep understanding of Quebec, for example, is balanced and sometimes overwhelmed in the scale of national politics by his inability to sympathize with the attitudes of other regions, particularly western Canada.

From my own experience, I know that it can take years for a Quebecer, even one whose mother tongue is English, to understand the origins of political opinions west of Ontario. It isn't a matter of learning about freight rates or the royalties paid on oil. Understanding starts by perceiving the different ethnic composition of western society, its history, and its appreciation of its own identity.

It takes a long time for someone from central Canada to accept the legitimacy of western objections to bilingualism, to understand that they arise not only from the prejudices that all Canadians share but from the common experience of living in a society where no man, ideally, is better than his neighbour merely because he speaks a different language. Discrimination based on language seems to contradict the democratic ideal that many European immigrants expected to find in western Canada. This desire for equality has to be appreciated by central Canadians whose history has given them a different tradition. It cannot be rejected simply as a "redneck" response to French Canada.

Trudeau is unable to understand this intellectually or to sympathize with it emotionally. He dismisses it as an alien, perhaps "American" concept of our society, mistakenly absorbed by western Canadians. His personal life as well as his political career bears witness to his lack of empathy for people who are guided by feelings rather than reason. He is not going to change now. He has spent fifteen years in Ottawa listening to western Canadians, some of them in his own party, and he gives no indication of having heard a word that they have said.

By now he regards the West as hostile territory. Voters there have repudiated him repeatedly and the antipathy is mutual. He has never taken kindly to criticism or defeat. He keeps his enemies as tenaciously as he retains those colleagues who appear to have served him well. Western Canada has never been, in our lifetime, as poorly represented in Ottawa as it is now, under a Prime Minister whose inability to understand or move the pride of westerners has been conclusively demonstrated.

The voice of the West is heard in Ottawa in the opposition parties and in the opposition of the four western premiers in negotiations with the Prime Minister. As a negotiator, Trudeau is skilled in all the arts except the most important, the ability to penetrate through the formal issues to the unstated feelings and expectations that underlie them. He is a masterful debater, but in a game where victory requires the co-operation of others, he often can't win. He can only try to control his impatience at the political manoeuvres of his opponents, control his competitiveness lest he create sympathy for them, and wait for the moment when he can compete publicly with them in a direct struggle for the minds and hearts of voters.

That moment seems to have arrived in the wake of the 1980 federal election and the Quebec referendum. It will pass just as swiftly, at least for Trudeau. He has to act while the memory of the referendum is fresh, while Premier Lévesque is on the defensive and before a new Premier, Claude Ryan, would have the opportunity to mobilize Quebec against changes that Ryan could never accept. Time is also running out for Trudeau himself, at least according to the retirement schedule he announced when he resumed the leadership of his party early this year. The "window" when action on the constitution is possible is incredibly small. It seems to be there now. If we miss this opportunity, it will go by so quickly it will be invisible and forgotten within a few years.

Trudeau's image changes as rapidly as political conditions. He entered our awareness in 1965 as a playboy-politician. Then he became a symbol of hope and reform. In 1970, during the October Crisis, he stood for the unity of Canada. During the past decade, he has seemed at times to be a symbol of division to many Canadians, standing in the way of compromise and accommodation. Now, at the outset of his current and purportedly final term as Prime Minister, he seems to have a mandate to use power decisively.

Bringing the constitution home, changing it in ways that he considers essential, may create strong tides of feeling in this country. For a time, positions may harden and divisions widen. It will require intuitive and sensitive leadership, as well as courage and ruthlessness, to lead us through this period, a combination of qualities that Trudeau has never managed to put together as Prime Minister. If Trudeau is going to succeed, we are going to have to trust him, as we trusted Prime Minister Pearson on the question of a new flag in 1967. But it was easier to trust Pearson, who knew intuitively that he could announce the abolition of the Red Ensign to a convention of the Royal Canadian Legion, and that once it was done, it would seem almost absurdly easy. Pearson understood us.

Trudeau's task is symbolic, as Pearson's was, but infinitely more complex. He will have to make us feel that he is acting for Canadians, not against us. He will have to make us feel that we share in his struggle to reach a specific and almost impossible goal, as we all shared in the marathon run across Canada that Terry Fox tried to complete in the summer of 1980.

When we talked then about Terry Fox and his struggle against cancer, when we watched him on television hopping on his good leg and swinging the artificial one forward, mile after mile, we seemed to talk almost as much about Canada as we did about cancer. Even when a recurrence of his disease forced him to give up his run at the Lakehead, Terry Fox's achievement was treated by us as a national victory. This crippled country must have seen in Terry Fox an image of itself.

To reach his goal, Trudeau will have to run as Terry Fox did with all his disabilities in evidence, with no time to slow down, with a compulsion and single-mindedness that will convince us that he is running for all of us.

12.
The Will to Succeed

At a meeting of First Ministers in Ottawa in the spring of 1980, Prime Minister Trudeau introduced a suggested preamble for a new constitution. It began: "We, the people of Canada . . . ." He never got past that point. Our federal and provincial leaders could not agree on the first five words of the proposed constitution.

In the sixties, we couldn't agree on whether we were citizens of one nation or two. In 1980, we were unable to describe ourselves even as the people of Canada. Surely the process of denying our national existence, at that point, went as far as it could go.

Quebec stumbled over the first few words of the preamble, but every province would have come to a halt before reaching the end. The idea of Canada as a coherent political and economic structure has been weakened so badly in the past twenty years that it no longer exists on paper or in the minds of many Canadians. Our generation has been sustained by little more than the sheer momentum of our history. We have contributed nothing to the strengthening of Canada.

Many of us now feel that this simply can't go on much longer. There has to be a new beginning. We have become desperate enough to accept almost any decisive move, even if it is largely symbolic. We believe that the process of bringing home the constitution will be valuable in itself, even if nothing else is done at this time.

There are many who say that simply patriating the constitution will be an empty gesture. If it is a move that has no importance, why has it been opposed so vehemently? Because its opponents recognize the symbolic power of the constitution. Bringing it home, they know, will be regarded as a landmark event in our history, a signal that we have reached a new stage of national development. And they also know that if we can hold true to this purpose in the face of opposition, it will have a profound effect on us. It will show us the way to greater achievements as a unified nation, and some of them fear that.

In an ideal world, Canadians would be able to accomplish this unanimously. That ideal is impossible for any country, but particularly for us. We have always been a divided nation except, for a brief moment, in the minds of some of the Fathers of Confederation. We have become so accustomed to our divisions that a great effort to surmount them seems to go against our nature. The claim is often made that we can best advance our own interests by doing nothing. That proposition is essentially what most of our provincial leaders have been saying for years. After twelve years of intermittent discussion of a new constitution under the guidance of Prime Minister Trudeau, they were still asking for more time in the fall of 1980. In the sixties, under Ontario's Premier John Robarts and Quebec's Premier Jean Lesage, it was the premiers who were a force for change. Now they are on the defensive.

Many of the most important premiers have now been in politics for what seems a long time – Davis of Ontario, Lougheed of Alberta, Lévesque of Quebec, Blakeney of Saskatchewan, Hatfield of New Brunswick. They were new faces in the sixties but now they are all within sight of the end of their mandates. One more term is probably as much as any of them expect. Within four or five years, all of them will likely be gone, along with the Prime Minister. Sitting around the conference tables with him now, they have nothing new to say. Over the years, they have discovered the narrow limits of unanimity among themselves. They know that only Trudeau can bring their endless discussions to a conclusion.

Perhaps there are some among them who would like to be remembered by history as his collaborators in this venture, but their own concerns prevent most of them from supporting him. Most of the premiers fear that co-operation with Trudeau will open them to charges in their own provinces of having sold out – the accusation that turned around Quebec Premier Robert Bourassa at the last moment in 1971.

Political interests are deeply involved. The unspoken reason for the premiers' reluctance to collaborate with Trudeau has to do with their own power. If Trudeau succeeds in bringing home and perhaps changing the constitution, it will vastly increase the power of those identified with the change: Trudeau himself, his party, and the central bureaucracy. The premiers would be at a disadvantage in future negotiations with Ottawa. To willingly accept this for the sake of the nation is probably asking too much from the premiers, particularly when many of them sincerely distrust Ottawa and disagree with the kind of federalism that Trudeau represents.

If there is to be change, Trudeau will have to initiate it himself, perhaps making a direct appeal to Canadians in the process, either in a referendum or in a national election. The elements of change depend on the method. In agreement with the premiers, the Prime Minister would be able to bring home the constitution and to reform it completely. In isolation from them, he may be able to make few changes, perhaps none at all.

The most important change would be a charter of rights. This would entrench basic democratic rights in our constitution for the first time rather than having them established by tradition, rulings of our courts, and decisions of our Parliaments. Language rights would also be included and perhaps the right of Canadians to own property and work anywhere in the country.

Over the past twenty years, the legal status of the French language has been greatly strengthened in the federal government and in some provinces. There have also been many practical changes to improve French-language schools and government services in the provinces. Among themselves, the premiers have agreed that second-language education should be provided in all provinces where numbers warrant. But there are objections, particularly though not exclusively from Quebec, to writing this into the constitution.

Quebec is understandably worried about recognizing federal authority over language and schools, concerns that have been vital to its survival in the past. In English-speaking Canada, Trudeau's proposal for a charter of language rights has been caricatured as an attempt to impose bilingualism from coast to coast. Both these responses spring from the historic confrontation between French and English in Canada, not from the reality of life in our country today. If a new constitution is to mean anything, if it is to close the door on the bitterness of the past and open the way for equal partnership between our two main language communities, it must contain protection for these languages in all parts of Canada. Most Canadians would agree with this. It is long overdue. It is the least that we can ask from this generation of political leaders.

If Quebec is expected to recognize constitutional limits on its jurisdiction over language, other provinces will have to accept curbs on their ownership and control of natural resources. In this area, as on language, we have to be skeptical about partisan references to history and extremist warnings about dire but unlikely futures. Although provincial ownership of resources in the three western provinces has been recognized for fifty years, the practice of sharing resource wealth has been established since Confederation. The right of the federal government to direct the national economy and to control the redistribution of wealth cannot be challenged simply because some provinces temporarily accumulate enough wealth to influence the course of national development.

Surely these two principles of cultural and economic development can be embodied in our constitution without driving either Quebec or Alberta out of the union. If they cannot be accepted by the politicians and bureaucrats who have tried vainly to negotiate agreement on them for decades, then we should find a way to express our opinion on them. We should not be afraid to face a referendum on these questions. We should take courage from the common sense that Quebecers showed when they had to make a choice. On these basic questions, I believe, we are united. In Quebec and across Canada, the "silent majority" is impatient of further delay in bringing home our constitution and will express its attachment to Canadian federalism if it is put to the test.

There are, of course, many in our democracy who will never join the rest of us in this. These are the separatists within each of our main national communities. They speak from conviction, often from idealism, but they are the victims of our past failures. What they really want is revenge; they cannot ever be satisfied. There comes a time when we have to ignore them, and this is the time. The separatists on both sides thrive on our weaknesses. If we have the courage to confront them, we will discover how thin on the ground they are. They will disintegrate into insignificance and be absorbed finally into the mainstream of our political development.

Language and resources are only two primary elements of a new constitution. Twelve areas of constitutional reform were discussed this past summer by federal and provincial ministers, including reform of the Senate and the Supreme Court. All are important and the literature on each is voluminous. However, this book is not a statement on specific constitutional reform but a polemic on the process and what it means to all of us. If we succeed in bringing home the constitution, the number of changes in the constitution itself will be small. Perhaps patriation alone is all that will be achieved. In any case, the process of reform will not end there.

Bringing home the constitution will not solve all our problems. It will give us confidence in our ability to deal with them.

I can think of nothing more fitting to conclude twenty years of agony and turmoil in Quebec. It would be a sign that the rest of Canada recognizes the changes that have occurred in Quebec and a symbol, for all Quebecers, of maturity in the rest of the country. It would make all of us feel that the intense political effort of the past decades, the exhausting preoccupation with our internal divisions, has not been utterly useless. This generation requires that symbol of achievement.

Patriation would also be a symbol of our ability to change, to confront our failures, to recognize our divisions, and to accept new ways of looking at ourselves. Surely this is at the heart of western Canada's discontent – the fearful resistance to change that has crystallized in other parts of Canada. Bringing home the constitution would be a sign to the West that the nation retains the ability to reform its institutions.

The central reason that the constitution has remained overseas is that we have not trusted one another. We have been unwilling to give up the protection, mainly symbolic, of a higher power that would arbitrate our differences and prevent us, in an extreme case, from tearing ourselves apart. Suspicion and fear of one another has been stronger than our embarrassment at remaining, as far as our constitution is concerned, a subject nation. Bringing home the constitution would be a symbol of trust among ourselves.

The opportunity is now clearly defined; the main objectives are before us; and the political techniques for achieving them are familiar to us. The only unknown element is the strength of our will to succeed. Do we have the imagination, the political courage, and the determination to make it happen?

In the months to come, either we will go forward or we will regress. We can't postpone the process. The safe middle-ground that Canadians traditionally stampede toward in any controversy has shrunk to almost nothing. As all Quebecers have done, although perhaps not in the same fashion, all Canadians are now going to have to choose sides.

If we fail, we will try to fool ourselves into believing that the challenge was not real. History won't be so kind. The referendum is now on the record as a specific response by a majority of Quebecers to the changes that have transformed their society in the past two decades, but that's only part of the answer. Now the rest of Canada has to be heard. We have to complete the questionnaire. We have to write our answer on the dotted line that stretches into the future.

13.
Battle Dispatches 1980-81

Since I started to write this polemic with a "wonderful feeling . . . that I am saying nothing new . . . that I am simply stating what is in all our hearts," the process of constitutional reform has gained momentum. There is now a resolution before Parliament to bring home the constitution with a charter of rights and a formula for amending the constitution in future. This attempt is having a profound effect on us. Never before have we dared to proceed so far. Our divisions have never been more evident.

Negotiations between federal and provincial leaders have reached an impasse for the time being. Provincial premiers have been unable to reach agreement among themselves even on the terms of their opposition to the unilateral move by Prime Minister Trudeau. Premier William Davis of Ontario is at odds with the federal leader of his own party and with the Conservative premiers of Alberta and Newfoundland. The leader of the Quebec Liberal Party disagrees with Prime Minister Trudeau. Divisions within Parliament are so severe that the government already has used closure to force the resolution on the constitution through the first stage of debate.

The parliamentary debate on the constitution has coincided with a federal budget that increases Ottawa's share of oil and gas revenues at the expense of oil companies and the provincial governments. Ottawa also has embarked on a program of gradual appropriation of a significant share of our foreign-owned oil industry, a move that will strengthen the federal government's political and bureaucratic control of resource development. The struggle with Alberta and other resource-rich provinces over the right to control not only these resources but the character of economic development in the western provinces is reaching a conclusive stage. Under this pressure, separatism in western Canada is emerging rapidly as a respectable political option of unknown potential.

Opposition to the Trudeau government's constitutional proposal has bridged many regional and language barriers, bringing together such disparate leaders as Quebec's Premier René Lévesque, Alberta's Premier Peter Lougheed, and the federal Conservative leader, Joe Clark. Quebec is one of a number of provinces taking steps to oppose patriation or at least to delay it in the courts.

To our surprise, embarrassment, and consternation, the fate of our constitution has become an issue in Britain. Canadian Indians have gone to London to enact a Victorian pageant in modern dress, asking the Queen, through the press and some members of her Parliament, to protect them from their own Parliament in Canada. Agents of provincial governments are lobbying British MPs to persuade them to obstruct the passage of the Canadian resolution in their own House.

Ironically, this attempt to sever the constitutional link with Britain is not only attracting attention to it but, at least for the time being, restoring its political vigour. For as long as most of us can remember, we have regarded this connection as a quaint curiosity; the British have appeared to agree with us. Now, because of our apparent inability to resolve constitutional issues on our own, we seem to be asking British parliamentarians to take sides in a dispute which they cannot possibly arbitrate. If this process continues, aided by the provinces and minority groups in our own country, it may make it difficult for Westminster to sever a connection that has been regarded by most Canadians up to this point as purely ceremonial.

At this moment, projected political scenarios flicker and shift like the Northern Lights in our winter skies. Some suggest that the charter of rights is a mere bargaining counter that Prime Minister Trudeau ultimately will trade for patriation with some form of amending formula. Others see, in the light of questions being raised in Britain about Trudeau's tactics, the possibility of a federal election or referendum campaign mounted as a crusade to liberate Canadians once and for all from their colonial bonds.

Whatever the future may hold, there is no doubt about the present mood of the country. We are paying a terrible price for decades of disunity and self-deception. Even at this point, when the die is cast, the will to persevere is uncertain. The limited confrontation that we have seen so far has frightened many Canadians. The national tendency, at this point, is to pause. The rationale for doing nothing gains adherents day by day.

There is no logic in this desire to procrastinate. Pleas for renewed federal-provincial negotiation on the constitution don't even pretend to be based on new evidence of co-operation between governments. Provinces that cannot unite to oppose patriation in the courts certainly will never come together under less duress. If the pressure for patriation and reform of the constitution is removed at this stage, the effort not only will come to a complete halt but will start to decay. Already we have gone too far, created too many expectations, and kindled too many strong feelings, for political life simply to return to normal, as if nothing had happened. Defeat would infect all of us with a sense of failure.

Still, many of us hang back. The reason most commonly given for hesitation is that this is not the way we have done things in Canada. This is a profound reaction in many Canadians who sense that we have managed our problems in the past by turning our backs on them and suppressing our true feelings. Delay and compromise have served the purposes of generations of Canadian politicians. It is difficult for many Canadians to reject what they have been taught to regard as the accumulated political wisdom of a century.

Confronting our regional differences, asserting our national will, pursuing national objectives even at the risk of testing the weakest points in our federation – admittedly, that is not the way we usually have done things in the past. That is precisely why we have reached this point-of-no-return in our history. The momentum of recent tradition is about to carry us over the brink unless we start to perform differently.

We have to rediscover an earlier tradition to regain our faith in the future.

The leaders who created our first Confederation clearly perceived a great nation arising from the partnership of English and French on the northern half of the continent. Some believed that one day it would surpass the mother country in wealth and influence – an impudent expectation at a time when Britain was the most powerful nation in the world. They shared a determination to build a homeland that not only might rival the United States but also might excel it in the strength of its institutions and the spirit of its people.

The vision of the Fathers of Confederation was equal to our vast resources. Today we possess territory that our ancestors only imagined as they pored over incomplete maps of our western and northern regions. We have discovered wealth beyond their dreams in our farms and forests, beneath the rocks of our northern tundra and the ice of our frozen seas. Our population is large by their standards but still relatively small. We have room to grow in a world where empty land has become one of the most valued assets. We seem to have everything except a clear idea of what to do with all this.

The grand vision of our ancestors has all but disappeared. We see the future as a series of diminishing vistas, as if we had long ago passed our prime as a nation. Disappointment has made us old in our attitudes and conservative in our expectations. As our actual potential expands in a troubled and hungry world, the nation or nations that we inhabit in our minds become, in our own estimation, smaller and more threatened.

Originally I intended to close this polemic by tempting Canadians with a new vision of the future, beyond the formidable economic and political difficulties that we can see in the short term. It would have been an easy task. Unlike most countries, we have all the basic elements of growth.

We have oil, natural gas, and coal in relative abundance – if we develop these resources carefully and use them wisely. Even as this is written, new discoveries of gas and oil are being made in the Arctic and off the coast of Newfoundland. If we schedule the development of these resources properly, we can aim realistically at self-sufficiency and enhance our competitive position in the world.

The development of our energy resources will require huge amounts of capital and manpower. Within a few years, the high unemployment that has acted as a constant drain on our economy will start to disappear. As unemployment declines, we will be able to look once again at the benefits of immigration. Population growth will encourage an expanding domestic economy.

Perhaps we even can expect larger Canadian families. The decline in our birth rate in recent decades may be a barometer of our political depression as well as the result of fashionable ideas about parenthood. The surge of energy and confidence that would accompany a political breakthrough in this country might well surprise and delight many Canadians in ways that seem to have little to do with politics.

With a strong central government that includes stronger representation in Ottawa from the provinces, with Ontario neither as dominant nor as resented as in the past, with Quebec committed to the federal union, we would be liberated from much of the dissension that has consumed our energies in the past. We could stop arguing and commence working together in an age that is coming to appreciate the importance of such traditional values as work, thrift, individual excellence, and strength of character.

We would also become a more tolerant society as relations between English and French settle into a new pattern. The warmth and friendship that often have existed between us as individuals, even when political hatreds were intense, hopefully would be expressed in our reformed political institutions.

It would have been easy, as I said, to portray this future in glowing detail, but the reasons for joining together now in an unprecedented act of national will lie elsewhere. They have to be found within ourselves.

I cannot accept the proposition, which opponents of constitutional reform are now putting to me, that I have been a member of a powerless generation in an insignificant time in our nation's history. I have witnessed too many changes in Quebec and elsewhere in this country to believe that. It flies in the face of everything that I have experienced.

The task of bringing home the constitution, no matter how flawed or incomplete the effort may be, is one that I instinctively and passionately share. Is it only symbolic, as its critics say? Well, I am starved for symbolism. I can remember how I felt when I first saw the flag in 1966 and when I heard the crowds in Montreal singing the anthem in 1980. I want more of that. I want that piece of parchment. Flag, anthem, and constitution.

"The World is as it is; men who are nothing, who allow themselves to become nothing, have no place in it."

V.S. Naipaul
A Bend in the River